Alex Anderson's
Hand & Machine
Appliqué

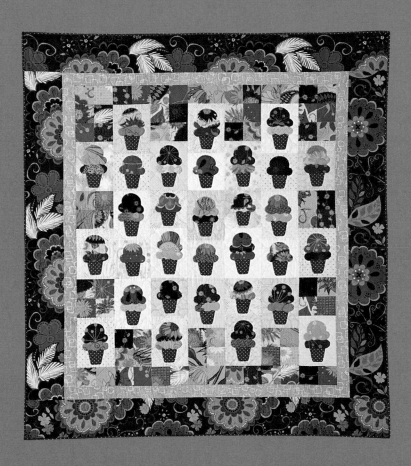

■ 6 Techniques   ■ 7 Quilt Projects   ■ Full-Size Patterns

C&T PUBLISHING

Text copyright © 2009 by Alex Anderson

Artwork copyright © 2009 by C&T Publishing, Inc.

Publisher: Amy Marson

Creative Director: Gailen Runge

Acquisitions Editor: Jan Grigsby

Editors: Liz Aneloski and Stacy Chamness

Technical Editors: Mary E. Flynn and Carolyn Aune

Copyeditor/Proofreader: Wordfirm Inc.

Cover Designer: Christina Jarumay

Page Layout Artist: Rose Sheifer-Wright

Book Designer/Design Direction: Kerry Graham

Production Coordinator: Zinnia Heinzmann

Production Editor: Alice Mace Nakanishi

Illustrator: Mary E. Flynn

Photography by Christina Carty-Francis and Diane Pedersen of C&T Publishing, Inc., unless otherwise noted.

Published by C&T Publishing, Inc., P.O. Box 1456, Lafayette, CA 94549

Library of Congress Cataloging-in-Publication Data

Anderson, Alex

Alex Anderson's hand & machine appliqué : 6 techniques, 7 quilt projects, full-size patterns / Alex Anderson.

    p. cm.

Summary: "Produce heirloom-quality appliqué by hand or machine without sacrificing either technique or artistry"--Provided by publisher.

ISBN 978-1-57120-611-4 (paper trade : alk. paper)

1. Appliqué. 2. Appliqué--Patterns. I. Title. II. Title: Alex Anderson's hand & machine appliqué.

TT779.A5247 2009

746.44'5041--dc22

                              2008046143

Printed in China

10 9 8 7 6 5 4

dedication

*To all the wonderful appliqué artists worldwide:
you've broadened and enriched my appliqué experience.*

acknowledgments

Thank you to:

P&B Textiles, who so graciously provided wonderful fabric to play with.

Bernina, who let me create and play with their terrific sewing machines.

Bob and **Heather Purcell** of **Superior Threads**, for their excellent products and for their dedication to educating the consumer about the wonderful world of thread.

Paula Reid and **Pam Vieira-McGinnis**, who helped me wiggle out of various tight spots as deadlines loomed.

Erica von Holtz, and her eagle eye.

Sandra Mollon, whose invitation to audit her class was the springboard for launching this project.

Darra Williamson, who was once again the guiding light behind this book.

Thank you, one and all!

contents

Introduction 4

The Right Stuff:
Tools and Fabric for Appliqué 6

Preparing for Appliqué 11

Hand Appliqué Techniques 19

Machine Appliqué Techniques . . . 24

General Instructions . . . 57

Resources 61

About the Author 62

the quilts

 Hearts and Flowers
28

 One Scoop or Two?
31

 Sweet Cherries
35

 Broken Dishes with Appliqué
40

 Nine Patch and Baskets
44

 Pomegranates
49

 Mix & Match Quilts I and II
55

introduction

I can remember when I took my very first appliqué class. The teacher wanted us to use the needle-turn method—that is, simply to turn the edges of the appliqué shapes under with the needle and stitch without basting or otherwise preparing the raw edges of the shapes. Please note that I use the word "simply" facetiously; there was absolutely nothing simple about this process for me. My hands had ten thumbs, and my appliquéd shapes were less than graceful.

As all good teachers do, my instructor took note of my struggles and adapted the lesson; she taught me to paper-baste over typing paper. (Now that dates me!) I loved both the process and the results, but I also recognized that hand-appliquéd quilts were neither for the faint of heart nor for the quilter looking for instant gratification. Nevertheless, I also understood that appliqué offered a means to an end that piecing did not—the opportunity to introduce free-form, curvy, organic shapes without the effort of matching points and joining seams—and that a combination of the two techniques could transform an ordinary quilt into a showstopper.

Since I first learned to appliqué, innovation in both technique and tools has blossomed, and nowadays appliqué is a snap! It is now possible to produce heirloom-quality appliqué by hand or machine without sacrificing either technique or artistry.

Whichever method you prefer, appliqué is a technique that needs to be in your quilter's tool belt. Originally I preferred hand appliqué, but I am now an avid machine appliquér as well. Believe it or not, the learning curve for machine work was minimal, and projects that would have taken me weeks (or months) to complete by hand, I now can do in a few days.

As you fall in love with appliqué, the best gift you can give yourself is to take classes with a variety of teachers. These don't need to be nationally known teachers at national shows—although that's good too. Explore classes offered by regional and local instructors at area quilt shops and quilt shows. Every appliqué artist has his or her own bag of tricks, and from that knowledge and experience, you can develop the methods that work best for you. Naturally, I have my own preferred tools and techniques—the tried and true that work for me—and those are the techniques that you'll find in this book.

Once you've read through the chapters on tools, the various methods of preparation for appliqué, and the different hand and machine appliqué techniques, and once you've determined which techniques you want to explore, choose one of the quilts in the project section and have at it. If you have never appliquéd before, you might want to start with *Hearts and Flowers* (page 28). This darling quilt is small and portable and covers many of the basics: bias stems, circles, and inner and outer curves.

So relax, enjoy, and have fun with the appliqué process, and remember: Rome wasn't built in a day, but perhaps your next appliqué project will be!

The Right Stuff:
Tools and Fabric for Appliqué

As with any art, craft, or trade, having the right tools and materials makes all the difference in the world. The following pages list and describe what you'll need for a successful appliqué experience.

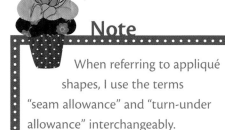

Note

When referring to appliqué shapes, I use the terms "seam allowance" and "turn-under allowance" interchangeably.

For most hand appliqué, your thread should match (or blend invisibly into) the color of your appliqué shape, not the background. The exceptions are reverse appliqué (page 23), for which the thread should match the over lying fabric, and the hand buttonhole stitch (page 22), which is intended to be visible and for which you might choose thread in a contrasting color as an accent.

 ## thread for hand appliqué

Many threads work well for hand appliqué. The most common is the 50-weight, 100% cotton thread you use in your sewing machine. It comes in a variety of colors, and you probably already have a good selection in your sewing box. However, there are *many* other threads you may want to try. The Rolls-Royce choice is silk, which buries itself so well in the fabric that you need only a few basic colors, such as light taupe, dark gray, and several primary hues. However, silk thread can be expensive; a wonderful alternative is a high-end 60-weight polyester such Libby Lehman's The Bottom Line (see Resources on page 61). Embroidery floss and perle cotton are good choices for hand buttonhole-stitch (blanket-stitch) appliqué.

thread for machine appliqué

With machine appliqué, you have two thread choices to make: the thread that passes through the needle of the machine and the thread that is wound on the bobbin. You'll also want to choose the best thread for the technique you plan to use.

Top thread: For the invisible appliqué stitch, use a high-quality invisible thread, such as Mono-Poly, or a fine 50-weight cotton, such as Alex Anderson's MasterPiece (see Resources on page 61), in a color to match the appliqué shape. Use jeans thread for the buttonhole (blanket) stitch. Your choice of color for the buttonhole stitch will depend upon whether you want the stitches to be inconspicuous or whether you want them to contrast with the fabric and thus act as a design element.

Bobbin thread: My favorite bobbin thread for the invisible appliqué stitch (including free-motion) is a fine cotton, such as MasterPiece, or a high-end polyester, such as The Bottom Line (see Resources on page 61). For this technique, the bobbin thread should match the color of the background fabric. For the buttonhole stitch, I prefer 50-weight cotton thread to match the top thread.

needles for hand appliqué

Various types of needles are available for hand appliqué, each with its own benefits. For the basic appliqué stitch (page 19), I recommend that you start with size 11 sharps, which are long, slender, easy to maneuver, and easy to find. Other options include straw or milliner's needles, which are slightly longer than sharps. If you are adept at hand quilting and are comfortable with a small needle, you might want to try a betweens quilting needle for your appliqué. For the hand buttonhole (blanket) stitch, choose a needle with a sharp point and an eye large enough to accommodate one strand of perle cotton or two strands of embroidery floss, such as a size 6–8 embroidery or sharps needle.

An important consideration when you choose a needle is the size of the eye. Is it large enough to thread without difficulty? Eye size can vary from brand to brand, so experiment to find not only which type but which brand of needle suits you best.

needles for machine appliqué

The topstitch needle is my hands-down favorite for all machine work—period. It suits a variety of threads, and I don't need to think about what I have in my machine when I sit down to sew. Its large eye is particularly kind to fragile (for example, metallic) and decorative threads. A jeans needle would be my second choice.

specialty feet for machine appliqué

If machine appliqué is your thing, you'll want to keep a few specialty sewing machine feet close by. For the invisible appliqué stitch (page 24), use an open-toe foot; it allows you to see where you are about to stitch and has a cut out "V" shape on the bottom that gives the stitch somewhere to go. The darning foot is the attachment of choice for free-motion appliqué (page 25). This foot allows you to steer the fabric, giving you—not the machine—control of the direction.

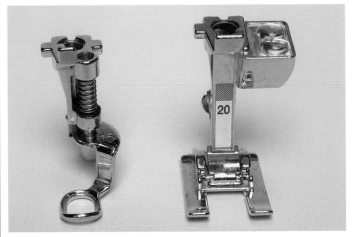

Darning foot and open-toe foot

pins

Don't skimp on pins! Look for pins that are short, sharp, and fine. Some quilters like the tiny sequin pins available at craft stores. My favorites are the extra-fine (1⅜"/0.50mm) glass-head pins I use for machine piecing. They are a bit more expensive than other pins, but—believe me—they are worth the investment. Avoid large, bargain-brand quilting pins; they'll get in your way, catching your thread as you sew and potentially leaving holes in your appliqués.

scissors

Keep three pairs of scissors on hand: one for cutting fabric, one for cutting paper and fusible web, and a small, sharp pair for snipping threads and other cutting.

marking tools

There are many options out there for marking on fabric, but my personal favorites are General's White Charcoal pencils, silver Verithin (any style) pencils, and extra-hard lead mechanical pencils. These simple tools allow me to mark a fine line that shows up on most fabrics, and the markings are fairly easy to remove. Whatever marking tool you select, test it first on fabrics you intend to use to be sure you can remove the markings.

heat-resistant template material

For shapes that must be traced multiple times, it's a good idea to make a template from sturdy material. Although cardboard or card stock will work, a much better choice is the translucent template plastic available at your local quilt shop. Choose a heavy, heat-resistant variety, particularly if you intend to use it for making circles.

freezer paper

The two sides of freezer paper—one with a dull, paper finish you can write on, the other coated with plastic that sticks to your fabric when pressed with a hot, dry iron—make it perfect to use for appliqué templates. You can purchase freezer paper by the roll at your local grocery store. Large (42″ × 42″) and small (8½″ × 11″) sheets are available from C&T Publishing (see Resources on page 61).

lightbox

Unlike many appliquérs, I do not mark the locations of the appliqué shapes on my background fabric. If a pattern is too complicated to arrange by using folded guidelines in the background fabric or by eyeballing it, I place the pattern on a lightbox and use the pattern to position the shapes, securing them to the background fabric with temporary, water-soluble fabric glue.

If you do not have a lightbox, you can substitute a sunny window, or you can place a lamp or flashlight beneath a glass-top table.

iron and pressing surface

Along with the full-size, all-purpose iron you typically use for your quilting projects, you'll find a mini (wand) iron—such as the Hobbico Craft Iron (see Resources on page 61)—extremely useful, especially for preparing appliqué shapes with the spray-starch technique (pages 12–13). A mini iron makes maneuvering those turn-under seam allowances *so much* easier!

> **tip**
>
> Some quilters reserve a separate iron just for use with their appliqué projects, particularly when these projects involve fusible web or spray starch.

For preparing your appliqué shapes, you'll want a really firm ironing surface so you can get a nice crisp fold on those turned edges. For pressing the finished appliquéd block, use a soft, giving surface, such as a fluffy towel folded double. Press from the reverse side of the block so you don't "smoosh" the appliqué shapes flat. (For pressing pieced blocks, I recommend a hard surface.)

temporary fabric glue

Look for a water-soluble temporary fabric glue, such as Roxanne's Glue Baste-It (see Resources on page 61), to secure your prepared appliqué shapes to the background fabric until you are ready to appliqué them in place. I use this glue for both machine and hand projects.

spray starch and brush

You'll need spray starch and a brush if you choose the spray-starch method (page 12) to prepare your appliqué shapes. You can use any generic spray starch found on the grocery store shelf, in either regular or extra strength. Be sure you use starch and not spray sizing, which doesn't seem to do the job as well. For the brush, you can use either a small paintbrush or a small foam makeup brush.

gluestick

Obviously, a gluestick is a must-have for the gluestick-basting method (page 14) of preparing your appliqué shapes. The brand is unimportant as long as the glue is water-soluble.

stiletto

A stiletto is a simple, sharply pointed tool that is essential for coaxing the seam allowance over the template when you are working with a mini iron to prepare appliqué shapes with the spray-starch method (page 12). Trust me: your fingers will thank you! My 4-in-1 Essential Sewing Tool by C&T Publishing (see Resources on page 61) includes a stiletto, a seam ripper, a pointed end for turning under the fabric edges, and a pressing tool.

pointed pressing tool

If you are using the spray-starch basting method, in addition to a stiletto, you'll want a pointed tool that is a bit thicker and heavier for preparing any deep inside ("V") angles. Again, the 4-in-1 Essential Sewing Tool is a good choice for this task.

lightweight fusible web

Fusible web is a heat-activated, synthetic fiber that, when placed between two layers of fabric and pressed, bonds the layers together. You can purchase fusible web in packaged sheets or off the bolt. Many brands are available; my personal favorite is Lite Steam-A-Seam 2 (see Resources on page 61). It is lightweight, it adheres but can be repositioned until pressed for a permanent bond, and it is easy to stitch through. Whichever brand of fusible web you select, make sure to read the manufacturer's directions for use (usually printed on the wrapper), particularly with regard to pressing.

stabilizer

Stabilizer, which is similar to interfacing, helps keep your machine buttonhole (blanket) stitches from puckering the fabric. Choose a tear-away version that you can remove easily after the appliqué shapes are stitched.

bias-tape maker

When used with your iron, a bias-tape maker is a handy notion that enables you to make folded bias strips from any fabric you like. The tool comes in various sizes, so you can make ready-to-stitch vines and stems in the width you need for your project.

bias presser bars

Bias presser bars are narrow bars, made from either metal or vinyl, that come in various widths—typically ⅛" to 1¾". Although the product name usually includes the word "bias," you can use them for stems cut from the straight grain as well.

fray check

Fray Check is clear liquid that helps stop fraying on the raw edges of appliqué shapes. (See Resources on page 61.) It is especially helpful when you are appliquéing very sharp inside ("V") angles, as for hearts and deep scallops, until you become confident with the security of your stitches. (Using a toothpick to apply the Fray Check will help you control the amount of the liquid.) As with marking tools, be sure to test it on the fabrics you intend to use.

fabric

As with any other quilting project, you'll want to put the very best fabrics into your appliqué quilts. If you are new to appliqué, I suggest that you start with *high-quality* 100% cotton fabrics—the kind you'll find at your local quilt shop. I can't stress the words "high-quality" enough. Trust me on this: you don't want to struggle with fabric that frays excessively or puckers or runs when the finished quilt is laundered. (Been there, done that—and I can guarantee, I wasn't smiling!)

As you become more adept, you might want to experiment with silks and other "exotic" fabrics. Some fabrics will prove to be stubborn; if you don't like how they handle, you are probably wise to avoid them.

Background fabrics set the mood; be sure they contrast strongly enough in value with your appliqué fabrics so your appliqués really shine.

Background fabrics for appliqué

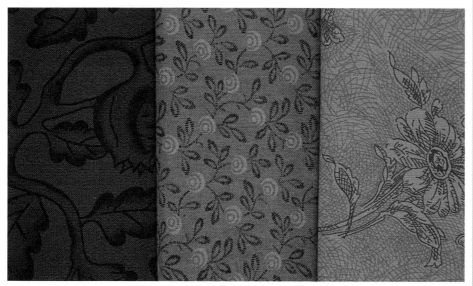

Tone-on-tone prints

"Sparkle" fabrics

If your appliqués are recognizable shapes (cherries, leaves, and so on), look for a variety of fabrics in the appropriate color. Avoid solids, especially if you are a beginner, because they tend to be unforgiving of less-than-perfect stitches.

Tone-on-tone prints and other subtle prints work well. Although usually monochromatic, these fabrics typically feature enough of a print to give you some cover for imperfection—an advantage when you are just beginning or are working to perfect your stitches. "Sparkle" fabrics—that is, single-color fabrics that include a range of values from dark to light—are great for creating special effects, such as the sunlight catching the dew on a leaf. Don't overlook the subtle shadings in hand-dyed fabrics. Just be sure to test the fabrics to make sure they are colorfast, or prewash them to remove any excess dyes.

One of the great benefits of appliqué is that you can cut your appliqué shapes and audition them on the background until you are happy with the effect, which offers lots of room for creativity and leaves the door open for last-minute changes.

If you typically don't prewash your fabrics, you may want to reconsider this practice for both hand and machine appliqué projects. Prewashing removes any sizing, finishing chemicals, and excess dye and makes the fabric more supple and the edges easier to turn. Also, some of the preparation methods involve the use of spray starch or temporary fabric glues that you will need to wash from the finished quilt.

Preparing *for* Appliqué

Appliqué takes a bit of preparation, both for the individual appliqué shapes and for the appliqué background. This preparation isn't difficult; read through the following pages to determine which methods will work best for you and your particular project.

preparing the individual appliqués

There are several ways to prepare the individual appliqué shapes. Some methods work for one specific appliqué technique, and others work for multiple techniques. Some methods are appropriate for handwork only, some for machine appliqué only, and others for both. To help you quickly identify an appropriate technique, I've accompanied each section with the appropriate icon of a needle and thread, a sewing machine, or both.

 ### Preparing for Needle-Turn Appliqué

1. To make a set of templates, trace each pattern given with the project onto sturdy template material. Cut out the templates on the traced lines.

Trace around template.

2. Place each template on the right side of the desired appliqué fabric. Trace around the template with your preferred marking tool.

3. Cut out the appliqué shape, adding a little less than ¼" (a "scant" ¼", approximately ³⁄₁₆") turn-under allowance.

Cut out shape.

Preparing for Paper-Basted Appliqué

You will need to reverse the pattern for paper-basting methods. When a shape will overlap with another shape, you do not need to prepare the raw edge that will be hidden. These raw edges will be indicated on the pattern with dashed lines.

Thread Basting

For the thread-basting method, the freezer-paper template remains in place while you stitch the appliqué shape to the background and is then removed after the stitching is complete (page 19).

1. Reverse the patterns given with the project, and trace them onto the dull (paper) side of freezer paper. You will need a freezer-paper template for each individual appliqué shape. Cut out the freezer-paper templates on the traced lines.

2. Place each freezer-paper template shiny side down on the wrong side of the desired appliqué fabric. Be sure to leave at least ½" between shapes to allow for the turn-under allowance. Press to adhere the templates to the fabric.

Place freezer-paper templates onto fabric and press.

3. Cut out the appliqué shapes, adding a scant ¼" (approximately ³⁄₁₆") for the turn-under allowance.

Cut out.

4. Roll the edges of the fabric over the freezer-paper template, and baste with a needle and thread.

Roll edge of fabric over freezer paper and baste.

Wrong side

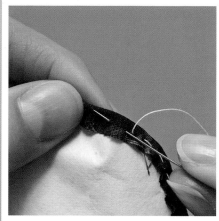

Right side

 Note

You must be willing to immerse the finished project in water to remove the spray starch because starch left in the fabric may attract silverfish.

 **Note**

For shapes with deep inside curves, use very sharp scissors to clip just to edge of the freezer paper. (Consider applying a drop of Fray Check to the fabric with a toothpick.)

Clip inside curve.

Basting with Spray Starch

*I **love** the spray-starch basting method; it has become my favorite way to prepare shapes for both hand and machine appliqué. Not only is it easy, but the freezer paper is removed before the shape is stitched to the background, so you can reuse the freezer-paper templates many times. Although you'll want to use one of the techniques described in Preparing Circles (page 15) to prepare your smallest round shapes, the spray-starch method works well for larger circles.*

1. Layer 2 pieces of freezer paper, shiny sides down, and press them so that the layers adhere to each other. The double thickness gives more rigidity and makes turning over the edges easier. Reverse each pattern piece given with the project, and trace it onto the dull (paper) side of the layered freezer paper. Cut out the freezer-paper templates on the traced lines.

2. Press the layered templates, shiny side down, to the wrong side of the desired appliqué fabric. Cut out the appliqué shapes, adding a scant ¼" (approximately ³⁄₁₆") turn-under allowance.

Press template onto fabric and cut out.

3. Spray a bit of starch into the cap of the starch can. (You can water the starch down a bit if you like.) Using a small paintbrush (or a foam makeup brush) and working with the paper side up, apply the starch to the exposed turn-under allowance. Be sure to use enough starch to saturate the fabric. (It's okay if you get some starch on the paper.)

Brush starch onto turn-under allowance.

4. Using a stiletto in one hand and a small wand iron in the other hand, coax the turn-under allowance over the edge of the freezer-paper template. When you are finished, turn the prepared shape over to check your results. Make any minor adjustments in the edges now; once the shape is thoroughly pressed (Step 6), you will not be able to make any adjustments.

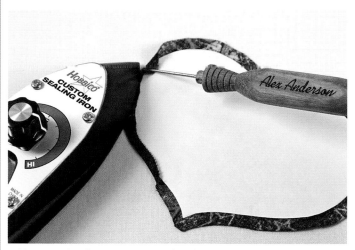

Fold turn-under allowance over template.

5. When you have finished turning the edges, press the prepared appliqué thoroughly on both sides.

6. Lift a small edge of the turn-under allowance, and remove the freezer paper. Re-press the appliqué to ensure that the starch is completely dry. Your appliqué is now ready to stitch, and you can reuse the template multiple times!

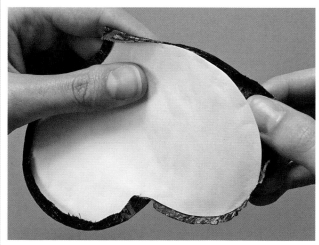

Remove template.

Gluestick Basting

Gluestick basting is another simple method for paper-basting appliqué shapes over freezer-paper templates. With this method, however, you will need to make one template for each individual appliqué shape. The template remains in place while you stitch the shape to the background and is then removed after the stitching is complete (page 19).

1. Prepare the appliqué shapes as described in Thread Basting, Steps 1–3 (page 12).

2. Using a water-soluble gluestick, apply glue to the turn-under allowance and roll the fabric over the paper template, using your fingers to maneuver the fabric smoothly over the edges of the template.

Apply glue and roll fabric over template.

Smooth fabric along edges with your fingers.

3. After you have appliquéd the shapes using your preferred hand or machine method, cut away the background, spritz the fabric with cool water to release the glue, and remove the template (page 19).

Here are some **tips** for coping with potentially tricky curves and angles when you use the spray-starch technique.

FOR CURVES

Don't try to press the entire curve in one motion. Instead, use the stiletto and the tip of the wand iron to create a ruffled edge around the curve. When you are satisfied that you have turned the curve cleanly, press the entire curve, and continue.

Finesse fabric around curve.

FOR DEEP INSIDE ("V") ANGLES

1. Use very sharp scissors to clip the fabric all the way to the edge of the paper template, directly toward the "V."

2. Place a pointed tool such as my 4-in-1 Essential Sewing Tool (see Resources on page 61) directly at the "V." Keeping the point nestled tight against the "V," pivot the tool's handle toward you.

3. Use the wand iron to carefully press the turn-under allowance in place on both sides of the "V."

Clip angle and press.

Preparing Circles

My favorite method for preparing circles for appliqué is the "shower cap" method.

1. Trace the circle pattern given with the project onto heat-resistant template material. Cut out the template on the traced lines. Go for perfection here; if the plastic circle is wonky, your finished fabric circle will be, too.

tip

Precut circle templates are available in a variety of sizes. You might want to check your local quilt shop or an on-line source for the sizes you need. Another option is to visit your local craft or scrapbooking store and purchase a circle cutter—it makes quick work of cutting your own templates from heat-resistant plastic.

2. Place the circle template on the wrong side of the desired appliqué fabric. Use your preferred marking tool to trace around the template.

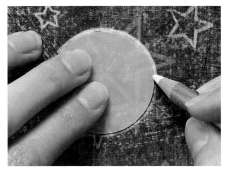
Trace circle onto fabric.

3. Remove the template and cut out the appliqué shape, adding a scant ¼" (approximately ³⁄₁₆") turn-under allowance.

Cut out.

4. Knot one end of a single strand of sturdy thread. Beginning with a backstitch, sew around the perimeter of the fabric circle with a running stitch, making sure to keep the stitching within the area between the traced line and the raw edge of the fabric circle.

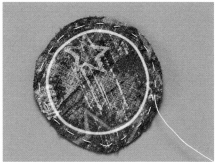
Sew.

5. Replace the template, and pull the thread to gather the fabric turn-under allowance around the template. Smooth out any folds, saturate the shape on both sides with spray starch, and use a *very hot steam* iron to press the fabric circle. Allow the starch to dry *completely.*

Pull thread to gather.

6. Loosen the gathering thread, and carefully remove the template. Once again, gently pull the gathering thread so the fabric forms a perfect circle.

Loosen thread and remove template.

  ## Preparing for Raw-Edge Appliqué

The raw-edge appliqué method is used to prepare appliqué shapes for hand or machine buttonhole (blanket) stitch. With this method, you do not add a seam allowance to the appliqué shapes. The shapes are prepared using a lightweight fusible web and are bonded to the background with an iron. As you did for the paper-basting preparation method, you will need to **reverse the pattern** *for the raw-edge appliqué method.*

OPTION 1 *Using a Template*

1. To make a set of templates, reverse each pattern given with the project, and trace it onto sturdy template material. Cut out the templates on the traced lines.

2. Follow the manufacturer's directions to bond the fusible web to the wrong side of the desired appliqué fabric.

3. Place the template on the paper side of the fusible web that you fused to the fabric in Step 2, and trace around the template with a sharp pencil.

Trace shape.

4. Cut out the appliqué shape on the traced line.

Cut out.

OPTION 2 *Tracing the Shape*

1. Reverse each pattern given with the project, and trace it onto the paper side of fusible web.

2. Cut out each shape approximately ¼" from the drawn line.

Trace shape onto fusible web and cut out.

3. Follow the manufacturer's directions to bond the fusible web to the wrong side of the desired appliqué fabric.

Fuse to fabric.

4. Cut out the appliqué shape on the traced line.

Cut out.

Preparing Vines and Stems

For curving stems and vines, cut strips on the bias (diagonal) of the fabric. Bias strips stretch nicely to create curves. For straight stems, which don't need to bend, you can cut the necessary strips from the straight (lengthwise or crosswise) grain of the fabric.

1. Use your ruler and rotary cutter to straighten the edge of the desired appliqué fabric. Place the fabric on your cutting mat, aligning the straightened edge of the fabric with a line on the mat. Position your ruler so that the 45° marking is aligned with the straight edge of the fabric. Make a cut.

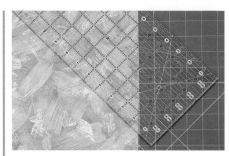

Position ruler and cut.

2. Move the ruler over to the cut width given in the project instructions. Line up the long edge of the ruler with the trimmed 45° fabric edge.

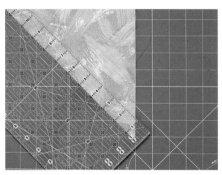

Position ruler.

3. Cut the strip. Continue cutting strips until you have the number (or total length) of strips required for your project.

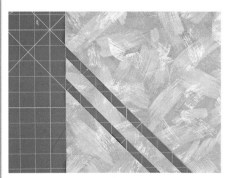

Cut.

When you are piecing multiple strips for vines, join the strips with diagonal seams as shown in Binding, Step 3 (page 60). Press the joining seams in one direction so the bias bar doesn't get hung up in the seam allowances.

Using the Sew-and-Flip Method

FORMULA Cut a bias strip twice the desired width of the finished strip plus ½".

1. Cut bias strips to the width and length listed in the project cutting instructions. With wrong sides together, fold the strip in half lengthwise, and press.

2. Hand or machine stitch the strip to the background fabric ¼" from the raw edges of the strip.

Fold strip in half, press, and stitch.

3. Carefully press the folded edge of the strip over the seam, so the strip covers the raw edges. If the strip is not wide enough to cover the raw edges, trim the seam allowance.

Press. Trim if necessary.

---

4. Use your preferred appliqué stitch to stitch the folded edge in place.

Stitch.

Using a Bias-Tape Maker

FORMULA Cut a bias strip twice the desired width of the finished strip.

Bias-tape makers come in a variety of sizes. Choose one that will give you the finished size you desire. My advice is to follow the instructions on the packaging of the bias-tape maker; however, here are a few tips to help you along.

- Cut the leading end of the strip at an angle so it is easier to feed into the tool.

- Spray the strip *lightly* with spray starch, and crumple the strip gently in your hands to distribute the starch evenly.

- Use a stiletto to maneuver the strip.

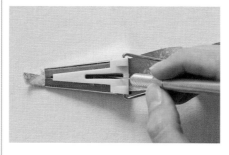

- Secure the angled end of the strip to the ironing board with a straight pin. With one hand holding the iron over the folded end, gently pull the tool across the fabric strip with your other hand, pressing the strip into shape.

- After you've used the tool, use straight pins to coax the prepared strips into gentle curves on your ironing surface.

Using Bias Presser Bars

FORMULA Cut a bias strip at least twice the width of the bias presser bar plus a scant ⅝" for metal bars and a generous ⅝" for vinyl bars.

1. Cut bias strips to the width and length listed in the project cutting instructions. If necessary, piece the strips with diagonal seams to achieve the required length as shown in Binding, Step 3 (page 60).

2. With wrong sides together, fold the strip in half lengthwise, and press. Carefully stitch ¼" from the long raw edge as shown to the left.

3. Insert the desired bias presser bar into the fabric tube, and roll the seam to the underside of the bar, trimming the seam allowance if necessary. Press the strip (I like to use steam). After each section is pressed, move the bar down the fabric tube, and press again. Take care if you are using a metal bias presser bar because it will get very hot.

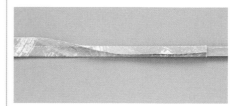

Roll seam to underside and press.

preparing the background for appliqué

I recommend that you cut your background blocks slightly oversize (1" or 2" larger in both length and width) to accommodate the slight shrinkage, or drawing up, that can occur as you appliqué the shapes.

1. Mark the center point of the background block and the vertical and horizontal (and sometimes the diagonal) axis points. These guidelines are extremely helpful in positioning the appliqués on the background area. You can mark the background block by folding it in half vertically and then creasing it with your fingers, or by using a pressing tool such as my 4-in-1 Essential Sewing Tool (see Resources on page 61) or an iron (lightly). Unfold the block, and repeat to fold and crease the block horizontally and, if desired, along both diagonals. You can also use the vertical/horizontal folding method to "mark" border strips for appliqué.

tip..

I do not mark the design on the background. Instead, I either eyeball the placement of the appliqués or use a lightbox to position and glue the appliqué shapes in place using temporary water-soluble fabric glue.

2. Layer the appliqué shapes from the bottom up, that is, in the order you will be stitching them. To help you, I've labeled the pieces for the project appliqués in alphabetical order, so you can place piece A first, then piece B, and so on. Place a few dots of the temporary fabric glue around the edges on the wrong side of each shape (and a few in the center, if you like), and gently finger-press the shape to the background.

Place temporary fabric glue.

3. Layer the shapes as appropriate.

Layer shapes.

tip..

When you are placing the shapes on the appliqué border for a square quilt (as in *Pomegranates* on page 49), arrange the motifs on one border, and then layer the remaining borders one by one to duplicate the arrangement.

4. Once you've finished with the appliqué, trim the block to the finished size *plus ¼" seam allowance* all around, making sure to keep the appliqué design centered in the block. The cutting instructions for the various projects allow for this seam allowance.

tip..

When preparing a motif with many layers (for example, the flowers in the border of *Broken Dishes with Appliqué* on page 40), it's a good idea to stitch the layers together before you appliqué the shape to the quilt top. Handling the small shapes in this way is easier than trying to stitch them individually to the larger quilt background.

Hand Appliqué *Techniques*

If you love the meditative quality of handwork, this is the chapter for you! Read through the options, choose an appropriate preparation method from the previous chapter, and enjoy the process. A small lap desk, like the type you might find in a book or stationery store, makes a great surface for hand appliqué. Make sure you have ample light, and stop occasionally to rest your eyes and stretch and flex your fingers.

basic stitch for needle-turn or paper-basted appliqué

For more-detailed information, refer to The Right Stuff (page 6).

- 50-weight, 100% cotton; silk; or high-end polyester thread to match or blend with appliqué shapes
- Size 11 sharps needle, straw or milliner's needle, or betweens quilting needle
- Small, sharp-pointed scissors
- Thimble (if you normally use one for hand sewing)
- Fray Check

PREPARATION METHODS Pages 11–18. Typically, if you are right-handed, you will stitch right to left, or counter-clockwise. Lefties usually stitch in the reverse direction: left to right, or clockwise. The photos show you both ways.

The following instructions for the basic appliqué stitch are the same for needle-turn or paper-basted appliqué. The difference is that with needle-turn appliqué, you turn under the seam allowances as you stitch the shapes to the background, whereas with paper-basted appliqué, the raw edges are turned under before you stitch the shape to the background. The instructional photos show the needle-turn method.

Note

If you have used the thread-basting (page 12) or gluestick-basting preparation method (page 14), you will need to remove the freezer-paper templates after the shapes have been stitched to the background. To do so, remove the basting threads, or moisten the shape to loosen the glue from the gluestick. Use small, sharp-pointed scissors to make a slit in the background fabric behind the appliqué shape as described in Cutting Away the Background (page 23). Remove the freezer-paper template. If you wish, cut away the background fabric inside the shape, leaving a scant ¼" (approximately ³⁄₁₆") seam allowance.

Left-handed

1. Thread your needle, knotting the end of the thread. The best place to start stitching is on a straight or slightly curved edge. Fold under the edge of the shape, on the marked line, where you will begin stitching. Turn under only the amount of fabric you can control and stitch at one time (about ½"). From the back of the shape, come through the fabric with the needle exactly at the folded edge you want to stitch. The knot will be hidden on the back of the fabric.

Right-handed

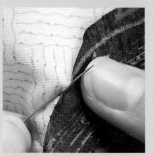

Left-handed

2. Reinsert the needle straight down into the background fabric, right beside the point at which the needle emerged. Travel approximately ⅛" under the background fabric, and then come back up again through the background fabric and the folded edge. Ideally, you want to catch the underside of the fold so the stitch is hidden under the fold. To complete the stitch, pull the thread just taut—not too tight, not too loose.

3. Continue using the tip of the needle to turn the edge of the fabric under as you go.

Right-handed

Left-handed

4. When you are finished stitching the appliqué shape, insert the needle straight down into the background fabric, and pull the needle so the thread is taut. Take a minute stitch in the background fabric behind the appliqué shape, as close as possible to the last appliqué stitch.

Right-handed

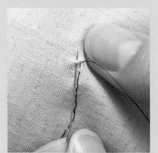

Left-handed

5. Wrap the thread around the needle twice, and pull the thread through the wraps.

6. Insert the needle through the background fabric between the appliqué and background layers, and come up about ½" from the insertion point. Trim off the thread. The tail will be hidden between the layers.

Right-handed

Left-handed

Curves

Use small, sharp-pointed scissors to clip the curved edge of the turn-under allowance, just to the marked line. The tighter the curve, the more clips you will need to make. As you appliqué the curve, make the stitches even closer together than usual.

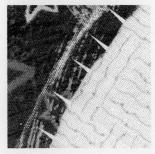

Right-handed

Points

1. Stitch up to the marked point using the basic appliqué stitch (pages 19–20). When you reach the point, bring the needle up through the background and the appliqué shape right at the tip of the marked point.

Left-handed

Right-handed

2. Take a stitch exactly at the point.

Left-handed

Right-handed

3. If necessary, carefully trim away a bit of the excess seam allowance underneath the area of the appliqué shape that you just stitched. The sharper the point, the smaller you will want the seam allowance to be.

Trim excess seam allowance, if necessary.

Trim excess seam allowance, if necessary.

4. Use the tip of your needle to gently turn under the seam allowance on the other side of the point. (Turning the seam allowance under completely at the point will require two or more turns.) Take an extra stitch to anchor the point, pulling the thread taut (not tight) to help define the point. Continue stitching away from the point with the basic appliqué stitch.

Left-handed

Right-handed

Inside ("V") Angles

1. Starting on a straight or slightly curved edge, use the basic appliqué stitch (pages 19–20) to begin sewing the appliqué shape to the background. Stop stitching just before you reach the "V," and use very sharp scissors to clip all the way to the marked turn-under line, directly toward the "V."

2. Take one or two tiny anchoring stitches right at the "V" to keep the clipped turn-under allowance from fraying.

Left-handed

Right-handed

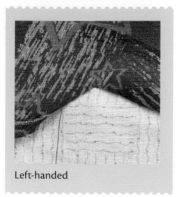

Left-handed

3. Resume stitching on the other side of the "V" with the basic appliqué stitch.

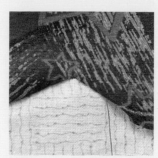

Right-handed

buttonhole-stitch (blanket-stitch) appliqué

For more-detailed information, refer to The Right Stuff (page 6).

- Embroidery floss or perle cotton thread in a color that contrasts with or matches the appliqué shape, depending upon the effect you desire

- Needle with a large eye and sharp point, such as size 6–8 embroidery or sharps
- Small, sharp-pointed scissors
- Thimble (if you normally use one for hand sewing)

PREPARATION METHOD Pages 11–18.

With buttonhole-stitch appliqué, there are no seam allowances to turn under, and the end result is less formal looking than that achieved with the needle-turn and paper-basting methods. You can choose threads to match the appliqués for a subtle effect, or have fun introducing threads in contrasting colors to add an extra layer of design.

Left-handed

1. Thread your needle with 1 strand of perle cotton or 2 strands of embroidery floss. Knot the thread.

2. From the wrong side of the background fabric, bring the threaded needle up through the background fabric at the raw edge of the appliqué shape. (The knot will be hidden behind the fabric.) Hold the thread against the fabric and away from the shape with your thumb. Insert the needle into the appliqué shape approximately ¼" from where the needle came out. Reemerge from the background fabric at the raw edge of the appliqué, bringing the tip of the needle over the working thread. Pull the thread taut (not tight) to bring the stitch into place. Continue stitching in this manner all the way around the shape.

3. Knot off as in Step 5 (page 20).

Right-handed

Left-handed

Points and Inside "V" Angles

When you reach a point or corner, make a small anchor stitch before proceeding to the adjacent side.

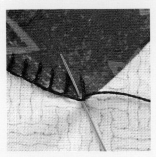

Right-handed

cutting away the background

Once a shape has been appliquéd to the background, you'll need to decide whether to cut away the background fabric from behind the shape. If the shape is small, dark, and only one layer deep, such as a small leaf, I tend not to bother. However, if the shape is multilayered, such as the flower in the border of *Broken Dishes with Appliqué* (page 40), or if an underlayer might shadow through, cutting away the background is a sensible step. Use small, sharp-pointed scissors to carefully make a slit in the background fabric behind the appliquéd shape. Cut away the background fabric inside the shape, leaving a scant ¼" (approximately ³⁄₁₆") seam allowance.

Cut away background.

reverse appliqué

When your appliqué design includes rounded shapes or shapes that should appear to recede—such as the circle cutouts in the bird in Mix & Match Quilt II (page 55)—reverse appliqué may be the answer. As its name implies, this easy technique is just the reverse of traditional appliqué. Rather than stitching the appliqué shape on top of another fabric, you layer the fabrics in such a way that when you cut away the top fabric in the desired shape, you reveal the appliqué fabric underneath.

1. Trace onto sturdy template material the pattern for the shape that you plan to reverse appliqué. Cut out the template on the traced lines.

2. Place the template on the right side of the *top* fabric, and trace around the shape with your preferred (non-permanent) marking tool.

3. Cut out the shape *inside* the traced line, leaving a scant ¼" (approximately ³⁄₁₆") turn-under allowance. Layer the top fabric over the right side of the fabric you want to reveal, and pin or baste.

4. Select thread to match the *top* fabric, and use the needle-turn method (page 19) to turn under and stitch the top fabric to the underlying layer.

Trace onto fabric.

Cut out.

Stitch.

Machine Appliqué
Techniques

When it comes to options for machine appliqué, "we've come a long way, baby!" With the innovations in sewing machine technology and with the wide variety of threads and notions available, machine appliqué is easier and more rewarding than ever.

invisible appliqué stitch

With just a little practice, you can give your machine work the look of beautiful hand-stitched appliqué.

Machines made by different manufacturers have different stitches to accomplish the invisible appliqué stitch. For example, on your machine, the stitch may be called the blind hemstitch, the over-lock stitch, the hand-look appliqué stitch, or something similar.

Refer to your machine's manual, and become familiar with what your machine can do. Don't be afraid to experiment. The key is to find a stitch that will take a few (two to three) small straight stitches along the outer edge of the appliqué shape and then take a bite into and out of the shape before continuing. You may want to shorten the stitch length and narrow the stitch width a bit; you want the bite to be as small as possible and still secure the appliqué shape.

I like to set my needle to the far right position and use the inside edge of the presser foot as a guide. Depending upon your machine, doing so may require that you mirror image the stitch.

PREPARATION METHODS Pages 11–18.

1. Attach the open-toe foot to your machine. Choose the appropriate stitch on your machine, and make any necessary adjustments.

2. Starting on a straight or slightly curved edge, position the needle right over the spot where you plan to start stitching. Lower the presser foot. Holding onto the top thread, take one complete stitch, so the needle returns to its highest position. In the following photographs, contrasting thread was used so stitches would be visible. Your thread should match your appliqué shape.

Take one complete stitch.

For more-detailed information, refer to The Right Stuff (page 6).

- High-quality invisible thread or a fine cotton thread in a color to match the appliqué shape for the top thread. (In the following photographs, contrasting thread was used so stitches would be visible.)
- Fine cotton thread or a high-end polyester thread to match the background fabric for the bobbin
- Topstitch or jeans needle
- Open-toe foot
- Small, sharp-pointed scissors

3. Without raising the presser foot, gently tug the top thread to pull a loop of bobbin thread to the fabric surface. Pull the tail of the bobbin thread through to the surface.

Pull top thread to bring bobbin thread to surface.

tip..

If your bobbin hook has an eye, thread the bobbin thread through it. Doing so helps pull down the top thread, enhancing the look of the finished stitch.

4. Engage the needle-down feature, if your machine has one. Insert the needle into the background fabric right beside the shape, and begin stitching. The machine will take a few small straight stitches and will then take a V-shaped bite into the appliqué shape.

Stitch.

Points

For a point (or an outside corner), stitch right to the tip of the point, making sure to stop with the needle down on the *inside* edge of the appliqué, having taken the first half of the V-shaped bite. Lift the presser foot, pivot, lower the foot, and resume stitching on the other side of the point.

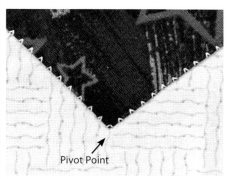

Pivot Point

Points

Inside "V" Angles

For an inside "V" angle, stitch right to the angle, this time making sure to stop with the needle down *outside* the edge of the appliqué shape, immediately after having taken the second half of the V-shaped bite. Lift the presser foot, pivot, lower the foot, and resume stitching on the other side of the angle.

Inside "V" angles

5. To end, pull the thread tails through to the back, and tie them off. OR reduce the stitch length and width to 0, take a few stitches in place, and carefully trim the thread tails. Your stitches may be visible at this stage, but they will become virtually invisible once the quilt is machine quilted.

free-motion appliqué

For more-detailed information, refer to The Right Stuff (page 6).

- High-quality invisible thread or fine cotton thread in a color to match the appliqué shape for the top thread
- Fine cotton thread or high-end polyester thread to match the background fabric for the bobbin
- Topstitch or jeans needle
- Darning foot
- Small, sharp-pointed scissors

PREPARATION METHODS Pages 11–18. Some years ago, I had the privilege of taking a private machine-quilting lesson with Margaret Gair, a marvelous local quilting instructor. As a bonus, she shared this terrific machine appliqué technique. It is a bit more time consuming than the invisible applique stitch method (page 24) but gives you more control. Rather than having the machine create the stitch, *you* manipulate the fabric to do what the invisible appliqué stitch does. Rather than creating a V-shaped stitch, however, you stitch in and out of the appliqué fabric with a tiny, straight-line bite. The smaller the bite, the finer the results.

You can do this free-motion work with the feed dogs engaged or dropped. Personally, I prefer not to drop the feed dogs for this technique. I feel that leaving the feed dogs engaged gives me more control.

1. Attach the darning foot to your machine. If you wish, drop the feed dogs. Pull up the bobbin thread and engage the needle-down feature, if your machine has one.

tip ....

If your machine has two spool pins (horizontal or vertical), and if the top thread is stacked on the spool, use the vertical spool pin. If the thread is cross-wound (crisscrossed), use the horizontal spool pin.

Cross-wound spool (left), stacked spool (right)

2. Starting on a straight or slightly curved edge, insert the needle into the background fabric right beside the raw edge. Take 2 or 3 straight stitches, and then take a tiny bite straight into and then out of the appliqué shape. Continue stitching.

3. Finish off as described in Invisible Appliqué Stitch, Step 5 (page 25).

raw-edge appliqué with buttonhole (blanket) stitch

For more-detailed information, refer to The Right Stuff (page 6).

- Jeans thread in a color that contrasts with or matches the appliqué fabric, depending upon the effect you desire
- 50-weight cotton thread to match the top thread for the bobbin
- Topstitch or jeans needle
- Open-toe foot
- Tear-away stabilizer
- Small, sharp-pointed scissors

PREPARATION METHODS Pages 11–18. The raw-edge appliqué with buttonhole (blanket) stitch technique for the machine has all the benefits of its hand counterpart. Experiment to find the stitch width and length that give you the desired result, keeping in mind the size of the appliqué shapes. If you prefer, you can substitute a satin stitch or one of the other decorative stitches on your machine for the buttonhole (blanket) stitch. Just make sure you choose a foot suited for the stitch.

1. Back the area behind the appliqué with a tear-away stabilizer to keep the stitches from puckering.

2. Attach the open-toe foot to your machine. Move the machine needle to the far right position, and select the buttonhole stitch on your machine.

Set the stitch length and width as desired, and if necessary, reverse the direction of the stitch. Pull up the bobbin thread, and engage the needle-down feature.

3. Starting on a straight or slightly curved edge, insert the needle into the background fabric, and begin stitching.

Stitch.

4. Finish off as described in Invisible Appliqué Stitch, Step 5 (page 25).

Points

1. For a point (or an outside corner), stop stitching as you approach the point, and use the hand wheel for control as you make the next few stitches. You may need to manipulate both the stitch *and* the background fabric a bit so the needle enters the fabric exactly at the point.

Stop stitching at point.

2. Leaving the needle in the down position, pivot the fabric, and take the bite stitch so that it divides the angle in half.

Pivot and make one stitch at point.

3. Return the needle to the background fabric, pivot, and continue stitching.

Inside "V" Angles

1. For an inside "V" angle, stop stitching when your needle enters the background fabric at the inside angle. Once again, you may need to manipulate both the stitch *and* the background fabric so that the needle enters at the correct place.

Stop stitching at inside angle.

2. Leaving the needle in the down position, pivot the fabric, and take the bite stitch so that it divides the inside "V" angle in half.

Pivot and make one stitch at inside angle.

3. Return the needle to the background fabric, pivot, and continue stitching.

Hearts
and Flowers

Finished quilt size: 33″ × 22″
Finished block size: 23″ × 12″
Skill level: Confident beginner

Designed, pieced, and appliquéd by Alex Anderson. Machine quilted by Pam Vieira-McGinnis.

Hearts and Flowers is a great little project for practicing or perfecting your appliqué technique. Originally created for a cruise in the Baltic Sea, it includes all the basics: bias stems, circles, and inner and outer curves. To make it even easier, I've included a layout of the full-size pattern on the pullout page at the back of the book. The layout will allow you to place the appliqués on the background fabric with accuracy and ease.

materials

Fabric amounts are based on a 42" fabric width. Fat quarters measure approximately 18" × 22".

- **Cream tone-on-tone print**
½ yard for appliqué background *

- **Green tone-on-tone print**
Fat quarter for vine and stem appliqués

- **Assorted green prints**
Scraps for leaf (A) appliqués

- **Assorted red prints**
Scraps for large heart (B), tulip (F and F reverse), and berry (G) appliqués

- **Assorted blue prints**
Scraps for small heart (C), tulip (D), and flower petal (H) appliqués

- **Assorted golden yellow prints**
Scraps for tulip (E) and flower center (I) appliqués

- **Golden yellow tone-on-tone print**
¼ yard for inner border

- **Red-and-blue print**
1 yard for outer border

- **Blue tone-on-tone print**
⅓ yard for binding

- **Backing**
⅞ yard of fabric

- **Batting**
38" × 27" piece

* You can piece the background from 2–4 assorted cream prints.

cutting

All measurements include ¼" seam allowances. Cut all strips on the crosswise grain of the fabric (selvage to selvage) unless otherwise noted. Appliqué patterns appear on the pullout page. Refer to Preparing the Individual Appliqués (page 11) for guidance as needed.

- **Cream tone-on-tone print**
Cut 1 rectangle 25" × 14". **

- **Green tone-on-tone print**
Cut bias strips to make vines and stems with a finished width of ⅜" (see pages 16–17).

- **Assorted green prints**
Cut a *total of* 10 piece A.

- **Assorted red prints**
Cut a *total of* 1 piece B.

Cut a *total of* 1 each of piece F and piece F reverse.

Cut a *total of* 3 piece G.

- **Assorted blue prints**
Cut a *total of* 1 piece C.

Cut a *total of* 1 piece D.

Cut a *total of* 8 piece H.

- **Assorted golden yellow prints**
Cut a *total of* 1 piece E.

Cut a *total of* 2 piece I.

- **Golden yellow tone-on-tone print**
Cut 2 strips 1¼" × 12½".

Cut 2 strips 1¼" × 25".

- **Red-and-blue print**
Cut 2 strips 4½" × 14" from the *lengthwise grain.*

Cut 2 strips 4½" × 33" from the *lengthwise grain.*

- **Blue tone-on-tone print**
Cut 4 strips 2⅛" × the fabric width.

** *This rectangle is cut slightly oversize and will be trimmed when the appliqué is complete.*

appliquéing the blocks

Refer to Preparing for Appliqué (page 11) and to Hand Appliqué Techniques (page 19) or Machine Appliqué Techniques (page 24) for guidance as needed.

1. Prepare 2 stems 7" long and 1 stem 2" long using the green bias strips.

Appliqué Placement

OPTION 1

See the sidebar on page 30 for an interesting appliqué placement option.

OPTION 2

1. Fold the 25" × 14" cream rectangle in half horizontally and vertically. Finger press.

2. Position the bias vines and stem from Step 1, 10 leaf (A) appliqués, 1 large heart (B) appliqué, 1 small heart (C) appliqué, 1 of each tulip (D, E, F, and F reverse) appliqué, 3 berry (G) appliqués, 8 flower petal (H) appliqués, and 2 flower center (I) appliqués on the cream rectangle as shown. Use your preferred method to appliqué the shapes in place.

3. Trim the block to 23½" × 12½", making sure to keep the appliqué centered in the block.

assembling the quilt

1. Refer to Butted Borders (page 58). Sew the 1¼" × 12½" golden yellow strips to the sides of the quilt. Press the seams toward the border. Sew the 1¼" × 25" golden yellow strips to the top and bottom. Press.

2. Sew the 4½" × 14" red-and-blue strips to the sides of the quilt. Press the seams toward the newly added border. Sew the 4½" × 33" red-and-blue strips to the top and bottom. Press.

finishing

Refer to General Instructions (page 57).

1. Layer and baste your quilt, and then quilt as desired. Pam machine quilted in-the-ditch around each appliquéd shape and then quilted a 1"-wide diagonal crosshatched grid over the background of the appliquéd block. The outer border was quilted in a wide rounded cable motif.

2. Sew the 2⅛"-wide blue tone-on-tone strips together end to end with diagonal seams, and use the long strip to bind the edges.

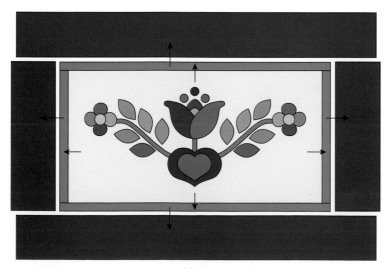

Assembly diagram

Using Quilter's Vinyl to Position the Appliqué Shapes

You can use Quilter's Vinyl (see Resources on page 61) or upholstery vinyl to help you accurately position the appliqué shapes.

1. Cut the vinyl (and its tissue-paper lining) to the finished size of the appliqué background. Save the tissue paper to store the vinyl pattern for future use.

2. Trace the appliqué pattern layout from the pullout page onto a sheet of paper, and then tape the paper onto a work surface. Tape the vinyl over the pattern.

3. Trace the pattern layout onto the vinyl with a fine-point permanent marker. Remove the tape from the vinyl.

4. Place the appliqué background fabric right side up on a work surface (a table for hand appliqué, an ironing board for fusible appliqué).

5. Place the vinyl right side up on top of the background fabric, matching the centers. Pin as needed.

6. Position the prepared appliqué shapes right side up in place, on top of the background fabric and under the vinyl, matching the pattern lines on the vinyl.

7. Pin the appliqués in place, or secure them with temporary, water-soluble fabric glue. For fusible methods, remove the vinyl, and fuse the shapes in place.

One Scoop
or Two?

Finished quilt size: 58½″ × 64½″

Finished block sizes: 6″ × 6″ and 6″ × 8″

Number of appliquéd Block 1: 10

Number of appliquéd Block 2: 21

Number of pieced blocks: 11

Skill level: Confident beginner

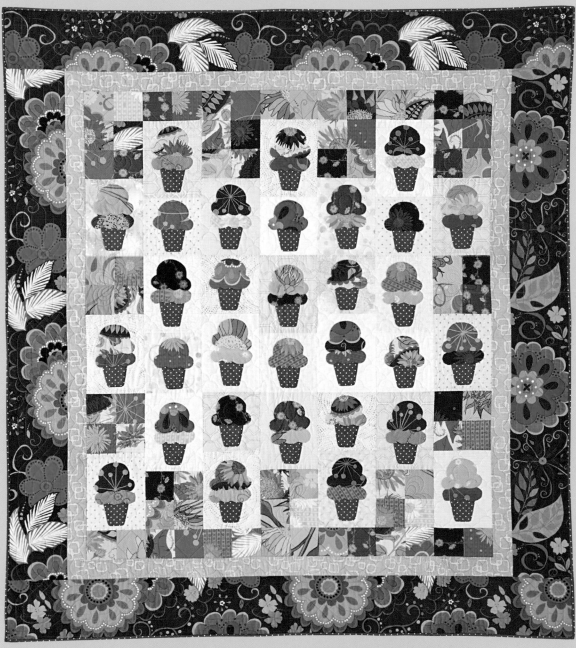

Designed, pieced, and appliquéd by Alex Anderson. Machine quilted by Paula Reid.

A while back, when well-known quiltmaker and shop owner Jean Wells was visiting, she handed me the most deliciously bundled stack of the latest fabric line designed by her daughter, Valori. The brightly colored prints were so yummy they made my mouth water just looking at them, and that's when the inspiration for this simple quilt popped into my head. You'll love it—and, unlike the real thing, it won't add an inch or a pound!

materials

Fabric amounts are based on a 42" fabric width.

- **White, cream, and beige tone-on-tone prints**
1¾ yards total for appliqué backgrounds

- **Brown-and-white polka dot print**
⅞ yard for ice cream cone (A) appliqués and binding

- **Assorted colorful prints in various print scales**
1½ yards total for ice cream scoop (B and C) appliqués, pieced blocks, and pieced border

- **Tan print**
⅝ yard for inner border

- **Large-scale print**
1¾ yards for outer border *

- **Backing**
3⅞ yards of fabric

- **Batting** 63" × 69" piece

* *You can use scraps of this fabric as one of the assorted colorful prints.*

cutting

All measurements include ¼" seam allowances. Cut all strips on the crosswise grain of the fabric (selvage to selvage) unless otherwise noted. Appliqué patterns appear on page 34. Refer to Preparing the Individual Appliqués (page 11) for guidance as needed.

- **White, cream, and beige tone-on-tone prints**
Cut *a total of* 10 squares 7" × 7". **

Cut *a total of* 21 rectangles 7" × 9". **

- **Dark brown-and-white polka dot print**
Cut 7 strips 2⅛" × the fabric width.

Cut 31 piece A.

- **Assorted colorful prints in various print scales**
Cut *a total of* 72 squares 3½" × 3½".

Cut 21 *total* of piece B.

Cut 31 *total* of piece C.

- **Tan print**
Cut 6 strips 2½" × the fabric width.

- **Large-scale print**
Cut 2 strips 6½" × 52½" from the *lengthwise grain*.

Cut 2 strips 6½" × 58½" from the *lengthwise grain*.

** *These squares and rectangles are cut slightly oversize and will be trimmed when the appliqué is complete.*

appliquéing the blocks

Refer to Preparing for Appliqué (page 11) and to Hand Appliqué Techniques (page 19) or Machine Appliqué Techniques (page 24) for guidance as needed.

1. Fold a 7" × 7" white, cream, or beige square in half vertically and horizontally. Finger press. Referring to the appliqué placement diagram below, use the creases to position 1 ice cream cone (A) appliqué and 1 ice cream scoop (C) appliqué on the background as shown. Use your preferred method to appliqué the shapes in place. Trim the block to 6½" × 6½", making sure to keep the appliqué centered in the block. Make 10, and label them Block 1.

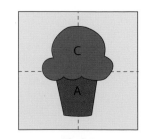

Block 1
Appliqué placement diagram
Make 10.

2. Fold a 7″ × 9″ white, cream, or beige rectangle in half vertically and horizontally. Finger press. Referring to the appliqué placement diagram below, use the creases to position 1 ice cream cone (A) appliqué and 1 of each ice cream scoop (B and C) appliqué on the block as shown. Use your preferred method to appliqué the shapes in place. Trim the block to 6½″ × 8½″, making sure to keep the appliqué centered in the block. Make 21, and label them Block 2.

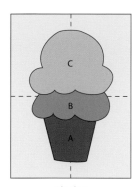

Block 2
Appliqué placement diagram
Make 21.

making the pieced blocks

Arrange four 3½″ × 3½″ assorted colorful squares as shown. Sew the squares into rows. Press. Sew the rows together. Press. Make 11.

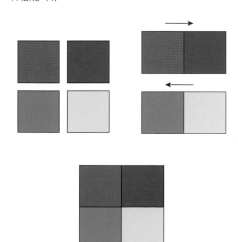

Make 11.

assembling the quilt

1. Arrange the appliquéd blocks and the pieced blocks in 7 vertical rows as shown in the assembly diagram below. Sew the blocks together into rows. Press the seams in alternating directions from row to row. Sew the rows together. Press.

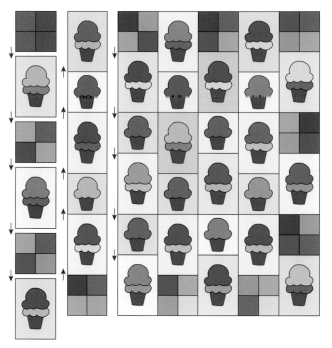

Assembly diagram

2. Sew 14 assorted colorful 3½″ × 3½″ squares together to make a row. Press. Make 2 rows. Sew 1 row to the top of the quilt and 1 row to the bottom. Press the seams toward the pieced rows.

Make 2.

3. Refer to Butted Borders (page 58). Sew the 2½″-wide tan strips together end to end to make one long strip. Press. From this strip, cut 2 strips 2½″ × 48½″, and sew them to the sides of the quilt. Press the seams toward the border. From the remaining strip, cut 2 strips 2½″ × 46½″, and sew them to the top and bottom. Press.

4. Sew the 6½″ × 52½″ large-scale print strips to the sides of the quilt. Press the seams toward the newly added border. Sew the 6½″ × 58½″ large-scale print strips to the top and bottom. Press.

finishing

Refer to General Instructions (page 57).

1. Layer and baste your quilt, and then quilt as desired. Paula machine quilted in-the-ditch around the shapes in each appliquéd block and filled the backgrounds with a small clamshell motif. She quilted each pieced block with a large pop-art flower design. The pieced borders were quilted in a square-within-a-square motif, the inner border was quilted with a simple roped design, and the outer border was quilted with an elongated double cable.

2. Sew the 2⅛"-wide brown-and-white polka dot strips together end to end with diagonal seams, and use the long strip to bind the edges.

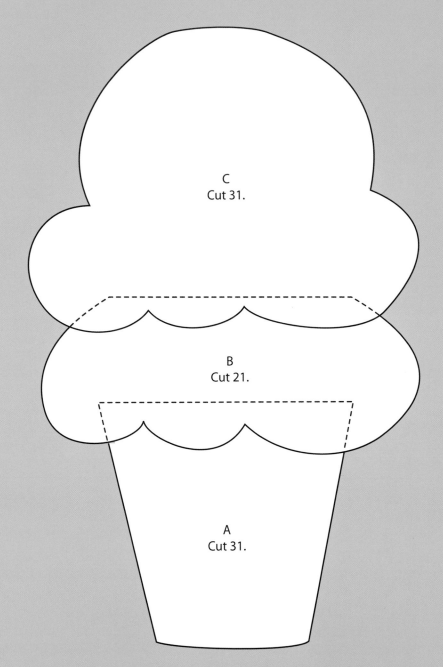

C
Cut 31.

B
Cut 21.

A
Cut 31.

Full-size patterns; no seam allowances included.
Reverse patterns for paper-basting or fusible methods.

Sweet Cherries

Finished quilt size: 41¼" × 41¼"

Finished block size: 10" × 10"

Number of appliquéd blocks: 4

Skill level: Confident beginner

Designed, pieced, and appliquéd by Alex Anderson. Machine quilted by Paula Reid.

Some of my best childhood memories are of summer holidays spent on my Gramma and Grampa's farm in Wisconsin. A highlight of every trip was the cherry picking. I can still taste those sweet, juicy treats—it's a wonder any fruit ever made it into the house! *Sweet Cherries*, with its four easy appliquéd blocks, recalls those lazy summer days. It's a great project for perfecting three appliqué basics: stems, circles, and outer points.

materials

Fabric amounts are based on a 42" fabric width. Fat quarters measure approximately 18" × 22".

- **White tone-on-tone print**
1⅜ yards for appliqué backgrounds, pieced blocks, and pieced units

- **Assorted pink prints**
¾ yard *total* for pieced blocks and pieced units

- **Hot pink mottled print**
⅜ yard for cherry (A) appliqués and flat piping

- **Green floral print**
Fat quarter for stem appliqués

- **Assorted green prints**
Scraps for leaf (B) appliqués

- **Black-and-white stripe**
¼ yard for inner border

- **Pink-and-white check**
1¼ yards for outer border

- **Black print**
½ yard for binding

- **Backing**
2½ yards of fabric

- **Batting**
45" × 45" piece

cutting

All measurements include ¼" seam allowances. Cut all strips on the crosswise grain of the fabric (selvage to selvage) unless otherwise noted. Appliqué patterns appear on page 39. Refer to Preparing the Individual Appliqués (page 11) for guidance as needed.

- **White tone-on-tone print**
Cut 4 squares 11½" × 11½". *

Cut 5 strips 3⅜" × the fabric width; crosscut into 40 squares 3⅜" × 3⅜". Cut each square in half once diagonally to make 2 large half-square triangles (80 total).

Cut 1 strip 4⅞" × the fabric width; crosscut into 3 squares 4⅞" × 4⅞". Cut each square in half twice diagonally to make 4 quarter-square triangles (12 total). You will have 3 triangles left over.

Cut 1 strip 2⅝" × the fabric width; crosscut into 9 squares 2⅝" × 2⅝". Cut each square in half once diagonally to make 2 small half-square triangles (18 total).

- **Assorted pink prints**
Cut *a total of* 40 squares 3⅜" × 3⅜". Cut each square in half once diagonally to make 2 large half-square triangles (80 total).

Cut *a total of* 3 squares 4⅞" × 4⅞". Cut each square in half twice diagonally to make 4 quarter-square triangles (12 total). You will have 3 triangles left over.

Cut *a total of* 9 squares 2⅝" × 2⅝". Cut each square in half once diagonally to make 2 small half-square triangles (18 total).

- **Hot pink mottled print**
Cut 4 strips 1" × 34¼".

Cut 48 piece A.

- **Green floral print**
Cut bias strips to make vines and stems with a finished width of ⅜" (see pages 16–17).

- **Assorted green prints**
Cut *a total of* 16 piece B.

- **Black-and-white stripe**
Cut 2 strips 1½" × 32¼".

Cut 2 strips 1½" × 34¼".

- **Pink-and-white check**
Cut 2 strips 4" × 34¼" from the *lengthwise grain.*

Cut 2 strips 4" × 41¼" from the *lengthwise grain.*

- **Black print**
Cut 5 strips 2⅛" × the fabric width.

* These squares are cut slightly oversize and will be trimmed when the appliqué is complete.

appliquéing the blocks

Refer to Preparing for Appliqué (page 11) and to Hand Appliqué Techniques (page 19) or Machine Appliqué Techniques (page 24) for guidance as needed.

1. Prepare 8 stems, each 9" long, using the green floral bias strips.

2. Fold an 11½" white square in half diagonally in both directions. Finger press. Referring to the appliqué placement diagram below, use the creases to position 2 bias stems from Step 1, 12 cherry (A) appliqués, and 4 leaf (B) appliqués on the block as shown. Use your preferred method to appliqué the shapes in place. Trim the block to 10½" × 10½", making sure to keep the appliqué centered in the block.

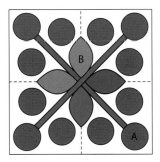

Appliqué placement diagram

3. Repeat Step 2 to make a total of 4 appliquéd blocks.

making the pieced blocks and units

1. Sew a large white half-square triangle and a large pink half-square triangle together along the long edges as shown. Press. Make 80.

Make 80.

2. Carefully noting their color placement, sew a small white half-square triangle and a small pink half-square triangle together along one short edge as shown. Press. Make 9 with the pink up and the white down, and make 9 reverse.

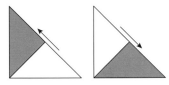

Make 9 each.

3. Arrange 16 units from Step 1 in 4 rows of 4 units each as shown. Sew the units into rows. Press. Sew the rows together. Press.

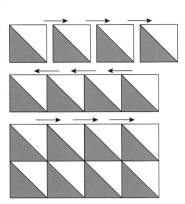

4. Arrange 10 units from Step 1 and 4 large white quarter-square triangles in 4 rows as shown. Sew the units and triangles into rows. Press, and label this Unit A.

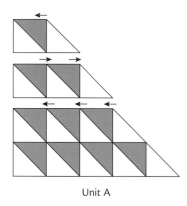

Unit A

5. Arrange 10 units from Step 1 and 4 large pink quarter-square triangles in 4 rows as shown. Sew the units and triangles into rows. Press, and label this Unit B.

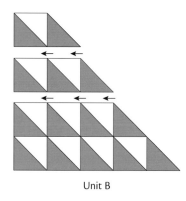

Unit B

6. Arrange 10 units from Step 1 and 4 units from Step 2 in 4 rows as shown. Sew the units into rows. Press, and label this Unit C.

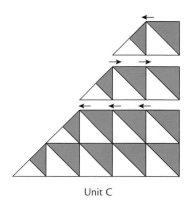

Unit C

7. Arrange 10 units from Step 1 and 4 units from Step 2 in 4 rows as shown. Sew the units into rows. Press, and label this Unit D.

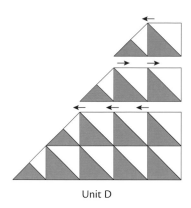

Unit D

8. Arrange 6 units from Step 1, 2 units from Step 2, and 2 large white quarter-square triangles in 4 rows as shown. Sew the units and triangles into rows. Press. Sew the rows together. Press, and label this Unit E.

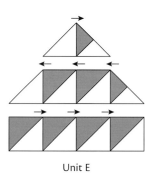

Unit E

9. Arrange 6 units from Step 1, 2 units from Step 2, and 2 large pink quarter-square triangles in 4 rows as shown. Sew the units and triangles into rows. Press. Sew the rows together. Press, and label this Unit F.

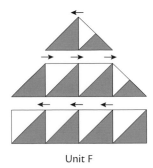

Unit F

10. Arrange 6 units from Step 1, 3 units from Step 2, and 3 large white quarter-square triangles in 6 rows as shown. Sew the units and triangles into rows. Press. Sew the rows together. Press, and label this Unit G.

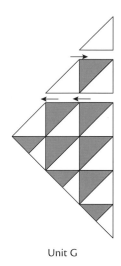

Unit G

11. Arrange 6 units from Step 1, 3 units from Step 2, and 3 large pink quarter-square triangles in 6 rows as shown. Sew the units and triangles into rows. Press. Sew the rows together. Press, and label this Unit H.

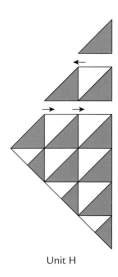

Unit H

assembling the quilt

1. Arrange the appliquéd blocks, pieced blocks, and pieced units in diagonal rows as shown in the assembly diagram below. Sew the blocks together into rows. Press the seams away from the appliquéd blocks. Sew the rows together. Press.

Assembly diagram

2. Refer to Butted Borders (page 58). Sew the 1½″ × 32¼″ black-and-white stripe strips to the sides of the quilt. Press the seams toward the border. Sew the 1½″ × 34¼″ black-and-white stripe strips to the top and bottom. Press.

3. Fold each 1″ × 34¼″ hot pink strip in half lengthwise, wrong sides together, and press. With right sides together and raw edges aligned, use a machine basting stitch and a scant ¼″ seam allowance to sew the strips to the sides, top, and bottom of the quilt.

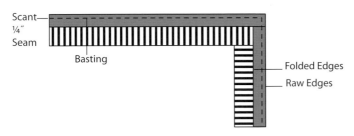

4. Sew the 4″ × 34¼″ pink-and-white check strips to the sides of the quilt. Press the seams toward the newly added border.

Sew the 4″ × 41¼″ pink-and-white check strips to the top and bottom. Press.

finishing

Refer to General Instructions (page 57).

1. Layer and baste your quilt, and then quilt as desired. Paula machine quilted a 1¼″-wide diagonal crosshatched grid over the surface of each appliquéd block and quilted in-the-ditch around each shape in the pieced block and pieced units, and along the seams of the inner border. The outer border was quilted in a feathered vine motif.

2. Sew the 2⅛″-wide black strips together end to end with diagonal seams, and use the long strip to bind the edges.

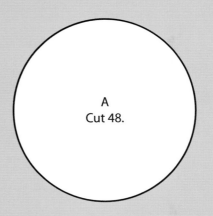

A
Cut 48.

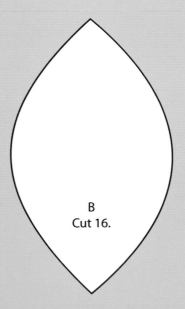

B
Cut 16.

Full-size patterns; no seam allowances included.

Broken Dishes
with Appliqué

Finished quilt size: 40½" × 40½"
Finished block size: 5" × 5"

Number of Broken Dishes blocks: 25
Skill level: Confident beginner

Designed, pieced, and appliquéd by Alex Anderson. Machine quilted by Paula Reid.

Sometimes a pieced quilt calls for appliqué as the superb finishing touch. That was certainly the case for this charming little wall hanging! I love the way the appliquéd flowers and vines complement the simplicity of the pieced Broken Dishes blocks. You'll love it too—the wall hanging goes together in practically no time at all.

materials

Fabric amounts are based on a 42" fabric width. Fat quarters measure approximately 18" × 22".

- **Assorted black prints and brown prints**
2 yards total for blocks and pieced outer border

- **Assorted yellow prints and orange prints**
1 yard *total* for blocks and flower background (B), flower petal (C), flower center (D), and bud (E) appliqués

- **Green tone-on-tone print**
Fat quarter for vine appliqués

- **Assorted green prints**
Scraps for leaf (A) and bud cup (F) appliqués

- **Golden yellow stripe**
⅓ yard for inner border

- **Black-and-brown print**
½ yard for binding

- **Backing**
2½ yards of fabric

- **Batting**
45" × 45" piece

cutting

Cutting directions are for two pieced blocks. Totals for the entire quilt are shown in parentheses. All measurements include ¼" seam allowances. Cut all strips on the crosswise grain of the fabric (selvage to selvage) unless otherwise noted. Appliqué patterns appear on page 43. Refer to Preparing the Individual Appliqués (page 11) for guidance as needed.

- **Assorted black prints and brown prints**

Cut *a total of* 13 squares 6¼" × 6¼"; cut each square in half twice diagonally to make 4 quarter-square triangles (52 total). You will have 2 triangles left over.

Cut *a total of* 68 rectangles 2½" × 6½".

- **Assorted yellow prints and orange prints**

Cut *a total of* 13 squares 6¼" × 6¼"; cut each square in half twice diagonally to make 4 quarter-square triangles (52 total). You will have 2 triangles left over.

Cut *a total of* 16 piece B.

Cut *a total of* 16 piece C.

Cut *a total of* 4 piece D.

Cut *a total of* 8 piece E.

- **Green tone-on-tone print**

Cut bias strips to make vines and stems with a finished width of ⅜" totaling about 180" in length (see pages 16–17).

- **Assorted green prints**

Cut *a total of* 24 piece A.

Cut *a total of* 8 piece F.

- **Golden yellow stripe**

Cut 2 strips 2" × 25½".

Cut 2 strips 2" × 28½".

- **Black-and-brown print**

Cut 5 strips 2⅛" × the fabric width.

piecing the blocks

1. Sew a black or brown quarter-square triangle and a yellow or orange quarter-square triangle along one short edge as shown. Press. Make 2 matching units.

Make 2.

2. Sew the 2 units from Step 1 together, carefully matching the center seams. Press.

3. Repeat Steps 1 and 2 to make *a total of 25 blocks*.

assembling the quilt

1. Arrange the blocks in 5 horizontal rows of 5 blocks each, turning the blocks as shown in the assembly diagram below. Sew the blocks together into rows. Press the seams in alternating directions from row to row. Sew the rows together. Press.

2. Refer to Butted Borders (page 58). Sew the 2″ × 25½″ golden yellow stripe strips to the sides of the quilt. Press the seams toward the border. Sew the 2″ × 28½″ golden yellow stripe strips to the top and bottom. Press.

Assembly diagram

3. Sew 17 assorted black and brown rectangles together along their long edges as shown. Press. Make 4 pieced borders.

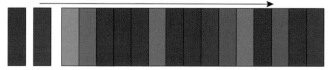

Make 4.

4. Refer to Partial-Seam Borders (page 58). Sew the pieced borders to the quilt. Press the seams toward the pieced border.

appliquéing the border

Refer to Preparing for Appliqué (page 11) and to Hand Appliqué Techniques (page 19) or Machine Appliqué Techniques (page 24) for guidance as needed.

1. Prepare 8 stems using the green bias strips.

2. Referring to the appliqué placement diagram below and the quilt photo on page 40, place the bias stems from Step 1, the leaf (A), flower background (B), flower petal (C), flower center (D), bud (E), and bud cup (F) appliqués on the outer borders as shown. Use your preferred method to appliqué the shapes in place.

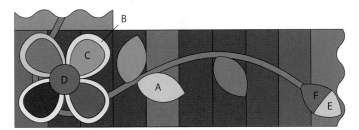

Appliqué placement diagram

finishing

Refer to General Instructions (page 57).

1. Layer and baste your quilt, and then quilt as desired. Paula machine quilted an overall large floral motif for the body of the quilt, lines of double zigzags in the inner border, and a wide cable in the outer border.

2. Sew the 2⅛"-wide black-and-brown strips together end to end with diagonal seams, and use the long strip to bind the edges.

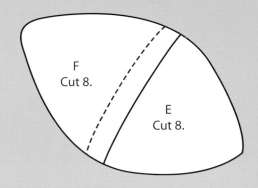

F
Cut 8.

E
Cut 8.

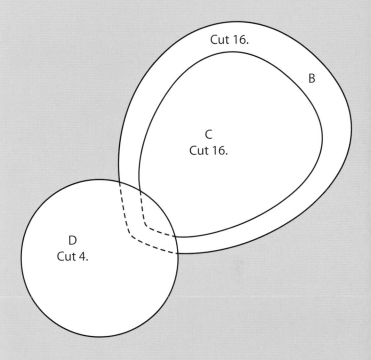

Cut 16.

B

C
Cut 16.

D
Cut 4.

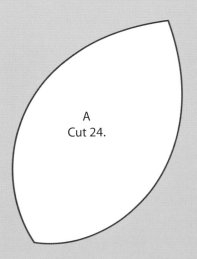

A
Cut 24.

Full-size patterns; no seam allowances included.

Nine Patch *and* Baskets

Finished quilt size: 66⅜″ × 72¾″
Finished block size: 4½″ × 4½″
Skill level: Confident beginner

Number of Basket blocks: 42
Number of Nine-Patch blocks: 56

Designed and pieced by Alex Anderson. Appliquéd by Alex Anderson and Gloria Smith. Machine quilted by Paula Reid.

There is nothing more inspiring than creating a new fabric line; the process is fascinating from beginning to end. Whenever one of my new fabric lines comes out, I make a quilt to play with all the fabrics. For my very first fabric line, a traditional Basket pattern proved the perfect showcase. Although I originally planned the border exclusively for "juicy" quilting, the finished quilt top seemed to cry out for appliqué, and my friend Gloria Smith came to the rescue. Once the appliqué was in place, Paula Reid worked her usual magic with exquisite quilting.

materials

Fabric amounts are based on a 42" fabric width.

- **White solid or tone-on-tone print**
5¼ yards for Basket block and border appliqué backgrounds, Nine-Patch blocks, setting triangles, pieced borders, and binding

- **Assorted colorful tone-on-tone prints**
3 yards *total* for basket (A), flower (B), and flower center (C) appliqués, Nine-Patch blocks, and pieced borders

- **Green tone-on-tone print**
¾ yard for vine and stem appliqués

- **Assorted green tone-on-tone prints**
Scraps for leaf (D) appliqués

- **Backing**
4 yards of fabric (horizontal seam) or 4⅜ yards (vertical seam)

- **Batting** 71" × 77" piece

cutting

Cutting directions are for one pieced block. Totals for the entire quilt are shown in parentheses. All measurements include ¼" seam allowances. Cut all strips on the crosswise grain of the fabric (selvage to selvage) unless otherwise noted. Appliqué patterns appear on page 48. Refer to Preparing the Individual Appliqués (page 11) for guidance as needed.

- **White solid or tone-on-tone print**
Cut 2 strips 6⅞" × 55¾" from the *lengthwise grain.*

Cut 2 strips 6⅞" × 62⅛" from the *lengthwise grain.*

Cut 5 strips 2⅛" × 62" from the *lengthwise grain.*

Cut 6 strips 5½" × the fabric width; crosscut into 42 squares 5½" × 5½". *

Cut 12 strips 2" × the fabric width; crosscut into 224 squares 2" × 2".

Cut 2 strips 7⅝" × the fabric width; crosscut into 7 squares, 7⅝" × 7⅝". Cut each square in half twice diagonally to make 4 quarter-square triangles (28 total). You will have 2 triangles left over.

Cut 2 squares 4" × 4"; cut each square in half once diagonally to make 2 half-square triangles (4 total).

Cut 10 strips 3⅜" × the fabric width; crosscut into 106 squares 3⅜" × 3⅜". Cut each square in half twice diagonally to make 4 quarter-square triangles (424 total).

Cut 1 strip 2" × the fabric width; crosscut into 16 squares 2" × 2". Cut each square in half once diagonally to make 2 half-square triangles (32 total).

- **Assorted colorful tone-on-tone prints**
Cut 56 sets of 5 matching squares 2" × 2" (280 total squares).

Cut *an additional* 220 squares 2" × 2".

Cut *a total of* 42 piece A.

Cut *a total of* 36 piece B.

Cut *a total of* 36 piece C.

- **Green tone-on-tone print**
Cut bias strips to make vines and stems with a finished width of ⅜" (see pages 16–17), totaling approximately 300".

- **Assorted green tone-on-tone prints**
Cut *a total of* 24 piece D.

* These squares are cut slightly oversize and will be trimmed when the appliqué is complete.

appliquéing the blocks

Refer to Preparing for Appliqué (page 11) and to Hand Appliqué Techniques (page 19) or Machine Appliqué Techniques (page 24) for guidance as needed.

Fold a 5½″ × 5½″ white square in half diagonally in both directions. Finger press. Use the creases to position 1 basket (A) appliqué in the center of the square as shown. Use your preferred method to appliqué the shape in place. Trim the block to 5″ × 5″, making sure to keep the appliqué centered in the block. Make 42 blocks.

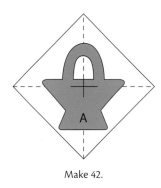

Make 42.

making the nine-patch blocks

Arrange 5 matching 2″ × 2″ colorful squares and four 2″ × 2″ white squares as shown. Sew the squares together into rows. Press. Sew the rows together. Press. Make 56.

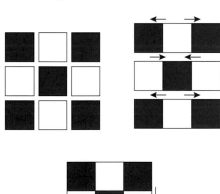

Make 56.

assembling the quilt

Arrange the Basket blocks, Nine-Patch blocks, large white quarter-square side setting triangles, and large white half-square corner setting triangles in diagonal rows as shown in the assembly diagram below. Sew the blocks together into rows. Press the seams toward the Nine-Patch blocks. Sew the rows together. Press.

Assembly diagram

making and adding the pieced borders

1. Sew a small white quarter-square triangle to opposite sides of a 2″ × 2″ colorful square as shown. Press. Make 204.

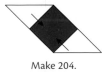

Make 204.

2. Sew 2 small white half-square triangles and a small white quarter-square triangle to a remaining 2″ × 2″ colorful square as shown. Make 16.

Make 16.

3. Sew 22 units from Step 1 together to make a row. Press the seams in one direction. Sew a unit from Step 2 to each end of the row as shown. Press. Make 2, and sew them to the sides of the quilt. Press the seams toward the pieced border.

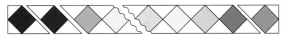

Make 2.

4. Repeat Step 3, using 21 units from Step 1 and 2 units from Step 2. Make 2, and sew them to the top and bottom of the quilt. Press.

5. Refer to Butted Borders (page 58). Sew the 6⅞″ × 55¾″ white strips to the sides of the quilt. Press the seams toward the border. Sew the 6⅞″ × 62⅛″ white strips to the top and bottom. Press.

Note

If you prefer, you can appliqué the borders before adding them to the quilt; see the sidebar under General Instructions (page 57).

6. Repeat Step 3, using 30 units from Step 1 and 2 units from Step 2. Make 2, and sew them to the sides of the quilt. Press.

7. Repeat Step 3, using 29 units from Step 1 and 2 units from Step 2. Make 2, and sew them to the top and bottom of the quilt. Press.

appliquéing the border

Refer to Preparing for Appliqué (page 11) and to Hand Appliqué Techniques (page 19) or Machine Appliqué Techniques (page 24) for guidance as needed.

1. Prepare 4 vines 50″ long and 24 stems 2½″ long using the green bias strips.

2. Referring to the appliqué placement diagram below and the quilt photo on page 44, place the bias vines and stems from Step 1 and the flower (B), flower center (C), and leaf (D) appliqués on the white borders as shown. Use your preferred method to appliqué the shapes in place.

Appliqué placement diagram

finishing

Refer to General Instructions (page 57).

1. Layer and baste your quilt, and then quilt as desired. Using the Nine-Patch squares as a guide, Paula machine quilted a 1½″-wide diagonal crosshatched grid over the center area of the quilt, including the baskets. She continued this grid into the pieced borders by quilting the border squares in-the-ditch. For the appliquéd border, she quilted in-the-ditch around each shape, and she enhanced the background with a feathered cable motif.

2. Sew the 2⅛″-wide white strips together end to end with diagonal seams, and use the long strip to bind the edges.

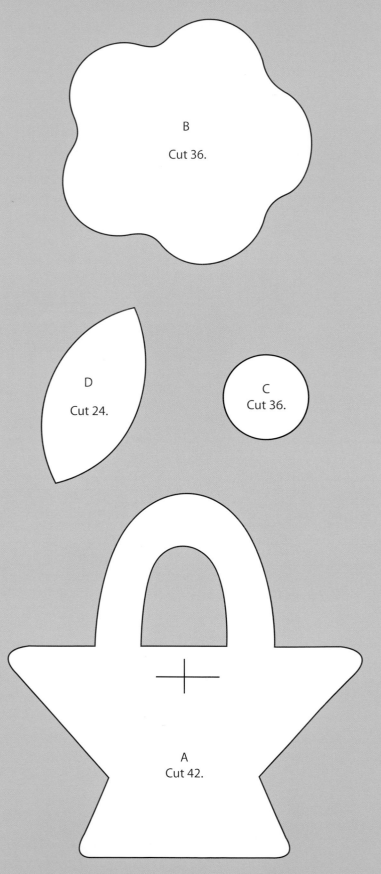

B

Cut 36.

D

Cut 24.

C

Cut 36.

+

A

Cut 42.

Full-size patterns; no seam allowances included.
Reverse patterns for paper-basting or fusible methods.

Pomegranates

Finished quilt size: 55¼" × 55¼"
Finished block size: 19" × 19"

Number of blocks: 4
Skill level: Confident beginner

Designed and appliquéd by Alex Anderson. Machine quilted by Paula Reid.

*P*omegranates is a deceptively simple but dynamic quilt that offers the perfect match of a beloved traditional pattern and snappy contemporary fabrics. The gently curved and rounded shapes are easy to work with, and the irregular swag border gives the piece a playful look. A nifty striped fabric provides a flashy finish.

materials

Fabric amounts are based on a 42" fabric width. Fat quarters measure approximately 18" × 22".

- **White solid**

3⅜ yards for appliqué background and border

- **Green tone-on-tone print**

1 yard for stem, leaf (A), and border flower (N) appliqués

- **Cheddar orange solid**

1⅜ yards for large flower (B), pomegranate (F), large swag (I), small swag (K), corner swag (M), and border flower (O) appliqués

- **Dark red solid**

1 yard for large flower (C), pomegranate (E), large swag (H), small swag (J), and corner swag (L) appliqués

- **Black polka dot on white background print**

⅜ yard for large flower center (D), pomegranate center (G), and border flower center (P) appliqués

- **Black-and-white stripe**

½ yard for binding

- **Backing**

3⅜ yards of fabric

- **Batting**

60" × 60" piece

cutting

All measurements include ¼" seam allowances. Appliqué patterns appear on pages 52–54. Refer to Preparing the Individual Appliqués (page 11) for guidance as needed.

- **White solid**

Cut 2 strips 9" × 38½" from the *lengthwise grain.*

Cut 2 strips 9" × 55½" from the *lengthwise grain.*

Cut 4 squares 20½" × 20½". *

- **Green tone-on-tone print**

Cut bias strips to make vines and stems with a finished width of ⅜" (see pages 16–17).

Cut 16 piece A.

Cut 20 piece N.

- **Cheddar orange solid**

Cut 4 piece B.

Cut 16 piece F.

Cut 8 piece I.

Cut 8 piece K.

Cut 4 piece M.

Cut 20 piece O.

- **Dark red solid**

Cut 4 piece C.

Cut 16 piece E.

Cut 8 piece H.

Cut 8 piece J.

Cut 4 piece L.

- **Black polka dot on white background print**

Cut 4 piece D.

Cut 16 piece G.

Cut 20 piece P.

- **Black-and-white stripe**

Cut 6 strips 2⅛" × the fabric width.

* These squares are cut slightly oversize and will be trimmed when the appliqué is complete.

appliquéing the blocks

Refer to Preparing for Appliqué (page 11) and to Hand Appliqué Techniques (page 19) or Machine Appliqué Techniques (page 24) for guidance as needed.

1. Prepare 16 stems, each 9" long, using the green bias strips.

2. Fold a 20½" × 20½" white square in half diagonally in both directions. Finger press. Referring to the appliqué placement diagram below, use the creases to position 4 bias stems from Step 1, 4 leaf (A) appliqués, 1 of each large flower (B, C, and D) appliqué, and 4 of each pomegranate (E, F, and G) appliqué on the block as shown. Use your preferred method to appliqué the shapes in place. Trim the block to 19½" × 19½", making sure to keep the appliqué centered in the block.

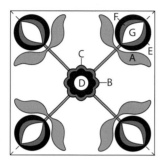

Appliqué placement diagram

3. Repeat Steps 1 and 2 to make a total of 4 appliquéd blocks.

assembling the quilt

1. Arrange the blocks in 2 rows of 2 blocks each as shown in the assembly diagram to the right. Sew the blocks together into rows. Press. Sew the rows together. Press.

2. Refer to Butted Borders (page 58). Sew the 9" × 38½" white strips to the sides of the quilt. Press the seams toward the border. Sew the 9" × 55½" white strips to the top and bottom. Press.

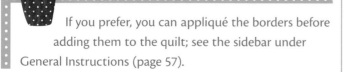

Note

If you prefer, you can appliqué the borders before adding them to the quilt; see the sidebar under General Instructions (page 57).

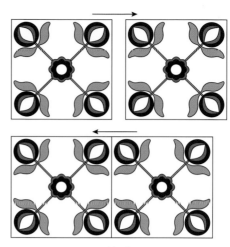

Assembly diagram

appliquéing the border

Refer to Preparing for Appliqué (page 11) and to Hand Appliqué Techniques (page 19) or Machine Appliqué Techniques (page 24) for guidance as needed.

Referring to the appliqué placement diagram below and the quilt photo on page 49, place the large side swags (H and I), the small side swags (J and K), the corner swags (L and M), and the border flower (N, O, and P) appliqués on the outer borders as shown. Use your preferred method to appliqué the shapes in place.

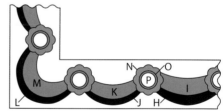

Appliqué placement diagram

finishing

Refer to General Instructions (page 57).

1. Layer and baste your quilt, and then quilt as desired. Paula machine quilted in-the-ditch around each appliquéd shape and filled the background and borders with a combination of ¾"-wide crosshatched diagonal gridwork, lush feathers, and echo swags.

2. Sew the 2⅛"-wide black-and-white stripe strips together end to end with diagonal seams, and use the long strip to bind the edges.

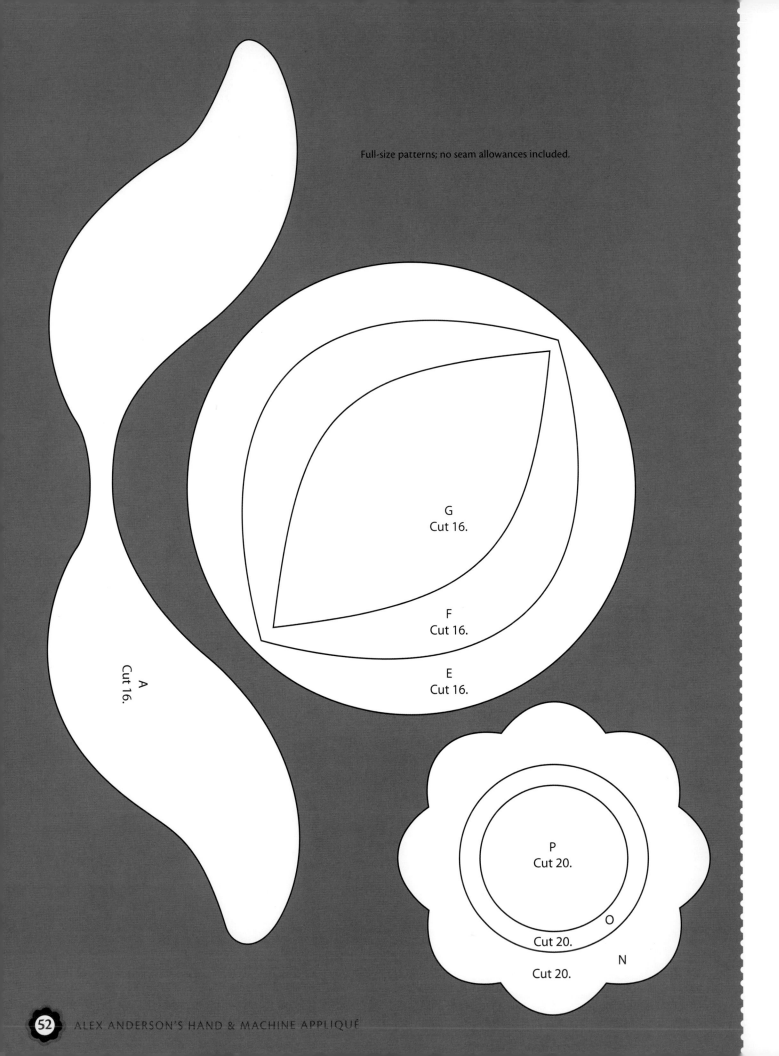

Full-size patterns; no seam allowances included.

G
Cut 16.

F
Cut 16.

E
Cut 16.

A
Cut 16.

P
Cut 20.

O
Cut 20.

N
Cut 20.

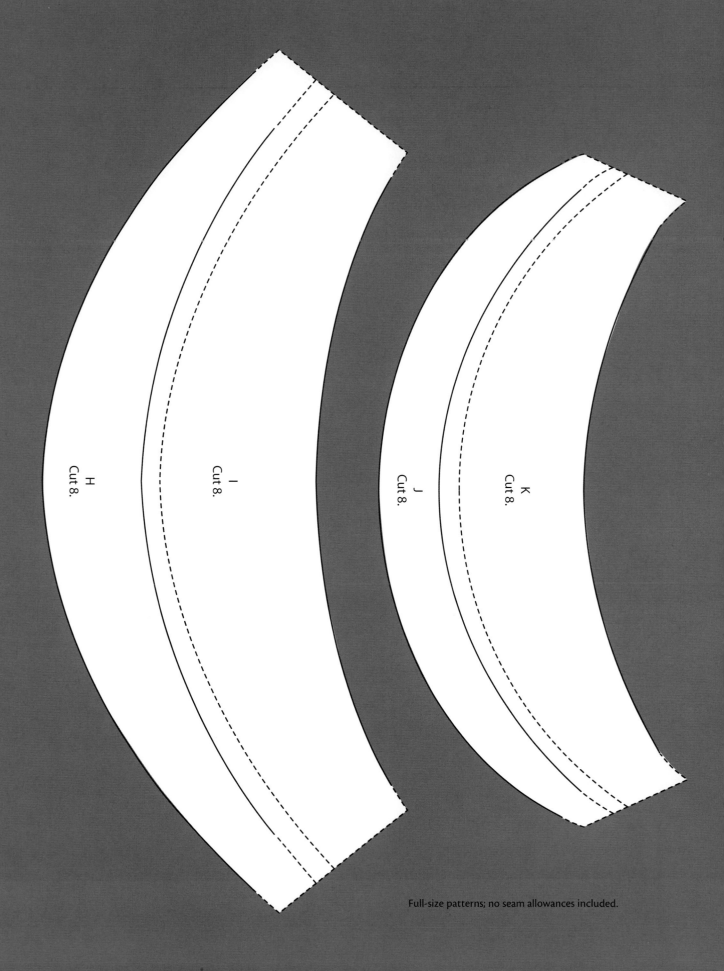

H
Cut 8.

I
Cut 8.

J
Cut 8.

K
Cut 8.

Full-size patterns; no seam allowances included.

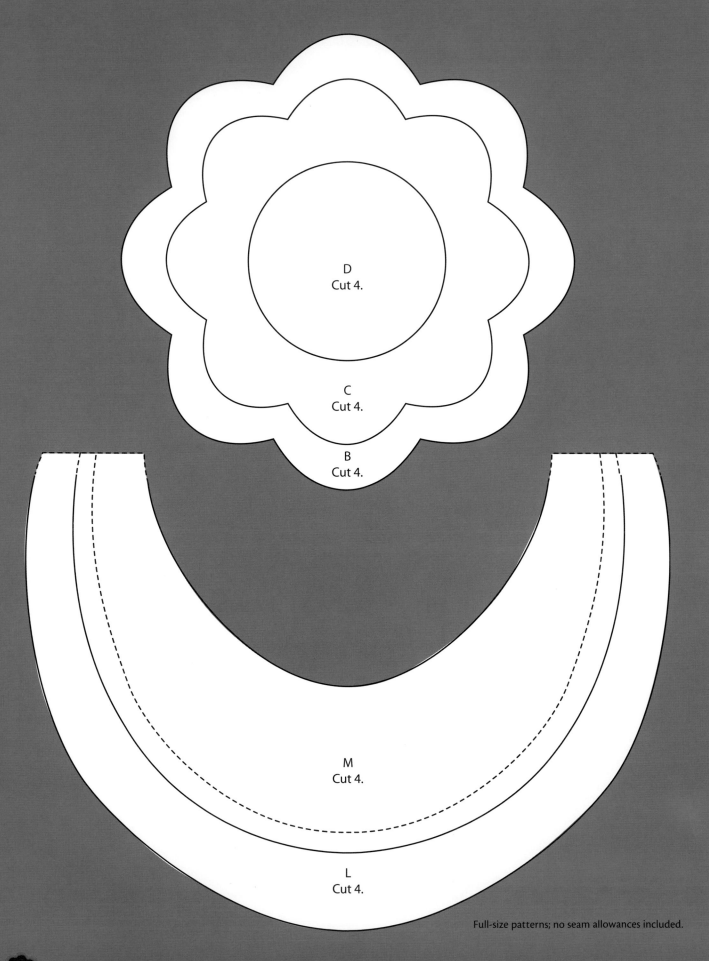

D
Cut 4.

C
Cut 4.

B
Cut 4.

M
Cut 4.

L
Cut 4.

Full-size patterns; no seam allowances included.

Mix & Match Quilts I *and* II

Finished quilt size: 19½" × 19½"
Skill level: Confident beginner

Designed, appliquéd, and machine quilted by Alex Anderson

*I*may be dating myself here, but when I was a little girl, I loved a toy called Colorforms. (The Barbie set was my favorite!) I was delighted with the freedom to create my own pictures by mixing and matching the colorful vinyl shapes however I wished.

Think of making these whimsical quilts as playing with your personal fabric Colorforms. Mix and match the shapes on the pullout page, or create your own (coloring books are a great source for simple shapes). Use the sample quilts as a guide for layout, or design your own compositions. No matter what your age, you're sure to be entertained!

materials

Fabric amounts are based on a 42" fabric width and are for one quilt.

- **Cream tone-on-tone print**
⅔ yard for appliqué background *

- **Green tone-on-tone print**
Scraps for stems

- **Assorted colorful prints**
Scraps for appliqués

- **Green tone-on-tone stripe**
⅓ yard for binding

- **Backing** ⅔ yard of fabric

- **Batting** 24" × 24" piece

* You can piece the background from 2–4 assorted cream prints.

cutting

All measurements include ¼" seam allowances. Cut all strips on the crosswise grain of the fabric (selvage to selvage) unless otherwise noted. Appliqué patterns appear on the pullout page. Refer to Preparing the Individual Appliqués (page 11) and Reverse Appliqué (page 23) for guidance as needed.

- **Cream tone-on-tone print**
Cut 1 square 21" × 21". **

- **Assorted colorful prints**
Cut appliqués as desired.

- **Green tone-on-tone print**
Cut bias strips to make vines and stems with a finished width of ⅜" (see pages 16–17); length and number of strips needed depend on your design.

- **Green tone-on-tone stripe**
Cut 3 strips 2⅛" × the fabric width.

** This square is cut slightly oversize and will be trimmed when the appliqué is complete.

appliquéing the block

Refer to Preparing for Appliqué (page 11), Hand Appliqué Techniques (page 19) or Machine Appliqué Techniques (page 24), and Reverse Appliqué (page 23) for guidance as needed.

1. Prepare stems using the 1¼"-wide or ¾"-wide green bias strips as desired.

2. Fold the 21" × 21" cream square in half diagonally in both directions. Finger press. Referring to the appliqué placement diagrams below or using the design and composition of your own choice, use the creases to position the appliqués on the square. Use your preferred method to appliqué the shapes in place. Trim the block to 19½" × 19½", making sure to keep the appliqué centered in the block.

Appliqué placement diagram

Appliqué placement diagram

finishing

Refer to General Instructions (page 57).

1. Layer and baste your quilt, and then quilt as desired. In each sample, I machine quilted in-the-ditch around each appliquéd shape and then quilted free-form swirly lines over the background.

2. Sew the 2⅛"-wide green stripe strips together end to end with diagonal seams, and use the long strip to bind the edges.

General Instructions

These instructions provide you the basics you need to construct your quilt.

rotary cutting

If you've never used a rotary cutter, you might want to read *Rotary Cutting with Alex Anderson* (see Resources on page 61). If the process is new to you, practice on some scrap fabric before starting on your project.

piecing

Set the stitch length on your sewing machine just long enough so your seam ripper will slide easily under the stitch. Backstitching is not necessary if the seam ends will be crossed by other seams.

pressing

You do not need to press the individual appliquéd shapes after you've stitched them to the blocks. Instead, press the entire block—I love to use steam for this—face down on a fluffy towel folded double.

When piecing, I usually press seams to one side or the other, but in some cases—for example, if six or more seams are converging in one area—I press the seams open to reduce the bulk. I've included arrows on the illustrations to indicate which way to press the seams.

There are two ways to appliqué borders

Sew the borders to the quilt top, and then stitch the appliqué shapes to the borders. For your first appliqué project or a small project, you might find this method the easier of the two.

Appliqué the borders before sewing them to the quilt top. You might prefer this method if the quilt is large, because a large quilt can be difficult to handle and because the border might shrink or become distorted as a result of the appliqué process. If you choose this method, cut the borders slightly larger (both wider and longer) than called for in the project instructions. Lightly mark a few guidelines to indicate the finished area of the border; stitch the appliqués, keeping them within the marked parameters; and then trim the border to the finished size plus the necessary seam allowances. If the appliqué design comes close to the end of the border strips, do not stitch down the appliqués at the ends of the border strips until after they have been sewn to the quilt top; then complete the corner areas of the design. If the design features a vine that turns the corner, you can split the vine and then add a corner motif, such as a flower, to cover the connection.

borders

The quilts in this book feature two different border treatments: butted borders and partial-seam borders.

Butted Borders

1. Measure your quilt top through the center from top to bottom. Trim 2 borders to this measurement, piecing them if necessary to achieve the required length. These will be the side borders.

2. Find and mark the midpoint on one side of the quilt top and the midpoint on one of the side borders. With right sides together, pin the border to the quilt top, matching the ends and midpoints and pinning every 2" in between, easing or stretching slightly to fit as necessary. Sew the border to the quilt top, and press as shown. Repeat for the other side border.

3. Measure the quilt top through the center from side to side, including the borders you just added. Cut 2 borders to this measurement, piecing them as necessary. Repeat Step 2 to pin and sew the borders to the top and bottom of the quilt. Press as shown.

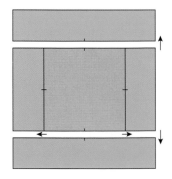

Partial-Seam Borders

1. Measure your quilt top through the center from top to bottom. To this measurement, add the finished width of the border, plus an extra ½" for seam allowances. Cut the side borders to this length.

2. Measure your quilt from side to side through the center. To this measurement, add the finished width of the border, plus an extra ½" for seam allowances. Cut the top and bottom borders to this length.

3. Find and mark the midpoint on each side of the quilt top.

4. From one end of each side border, measure and mark the *length* of the quilt top. Find and crease the midpoint between the end of the strip and the point you've just marked. Repeat for the top and bottom borders, measuring and marking the *width* of the quilt top and creasing to find the midpoint.

5. Place a side border and the right edge of the quilt top right sides together. Match the midpoints, then match the bottom right corner of the quilt top with the marked endpoint on the border, and pin. (The border will extend beyond the bottom edge of the quilt.) Align the opposite end of the border with the top right corner of the quilt, and pin as needed.

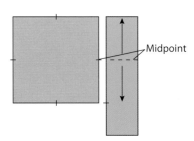

Midpoint

6. Stitch the border to the quilt top, stopping approximately 3" from the end of the border strip. Press.

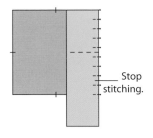

Stop stitching.

7. Place the top border and the top edge of the quilt top right sides together. Match the midpoints, then match the ends of the border with the corners of the quilt, and pin.

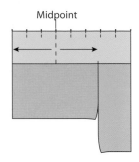

Midpoint

8. Stitch the top border to the quilt. Press.

9. Repeat to add the left side border and the bottom border.

10. Complete the first border seam. If necessary, trim and square the corners of the quilt.

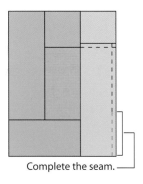

Complete the seam.

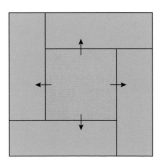

layering and basting

I typically cut my batting and backing 2″ larger than the quilt top on all sides. The amounts shown in the materials listing for each project include this extra "insurance."

Spread the backing wrong side up on your (nonloop) carpet or work surface. Smooth the backing, and secure it with T-pins or masking tape. Center the batting on top of the backing, and trim the two layers so the raw edges are even. Center the quilt top right side up on the batting, smoothing carefully to remove any wrinkles.

For hand quilting, use a needle and thread to baste the three layers together with large stitches in a 4″ grid pattern. For machine quilting, secure the three layers every 3″ with rustproof size No. 1 safety pins. Distribute the pins evenly, avoiding areas where you know you'll be stitching. For both hand and machine quilting, baste all the way to the edges of the quilt top.

quilting your appliquéd quilt

There are a few special considerations to keep in mind as you decide how to quilt your appliquéd quilt. For this reason, you'll probably want to begin thinking about potential quilting motifs and an overall quilting strategy right from the get-go.

A common option is to outline quilt each appliqué shape right along its outside edge. If an appliqué shape is particularly large, you also might want to add some quilting to the interior of the shape—another reason to cut away the background behind the appliqués. For the background areas (blocks and borders), straight-line designs, such as single or double diagonals or a grid, beautifully offset the curvy appliqués. You might also choose clamshells, fans, or other filler designs, depending upon the appliqué. Lush feathers are a great choice to weave around appliquéd vines in quilt border.

tip ....

For a vintage look, use crosshatching or another overall quilting motif over the entire surface, *including* the appliqués—a technique seen in many antique appliquéd quilts.

I love to hand quilt, but unfortunately, I don't always have time. I usually determine how the quilt will be used and then decide how to handle the quilting. Whether you hand or machine quilt, I have three thoughts to share:

1 *When it comes to quilting, more is better. Never skimp on the amount of quilting on your quilt.*

2 *Treat the surface as a whole. I often quilt my quilts with interesting grids that unify the design. However, I rarely quilt within ¼″ of the seam-lines, because this accentuates what to me is the most unsightly part of the quilt—the seams.*

3 *Use an equal amount of quilting over the entire surface. If you quilt different areas with unequal density, not only will your quilt look odd, but it will also sag and not lie flat.*

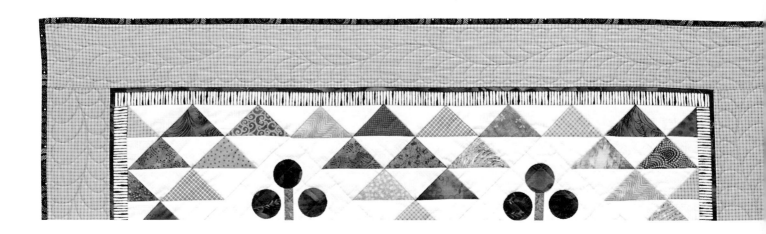

binding

1. Trim the batting and backing even with the raw edges of the quilt top.

2. Cut 2⅛"-wide strips from the fabric width as directed in the project instructions.

3. Sew the strips together end to end with diagonal seams, and press the seams open. Pressing this way will help prevent big lumps in the binding.

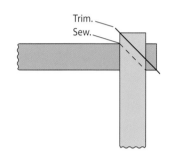

4. Fold and press the binding lengthwise, wrong sides together.

5. With raw edges even, pin the binding to the edge of the quilt, starting a few inches from one corner and leaving the first few inches of the binding unattached. Start sewing, using a ¼" seam allowance. For pucker-free bindings, use a walking foot or the even-feed feature on your sewing machine. Adjust the needle position to achieve the desired seam allowance.

6. Stop ¼" from the first corner, and backstitch one stitch.

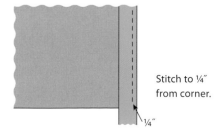

Stitch to ¼" from corner.

¼"

7. Lift the presser foot and needle. Rotate the quilt one-quarter turn. Fold the binding at a right angle so it extends straight above the quilt and forms a 45° fold at the corner.

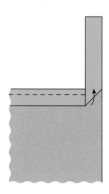

8. Bring the binding strip down even with the next edge of the quilt. Begin sewing at the folded edge. Stop ¼" from the next corner, and backstitch one stitch.

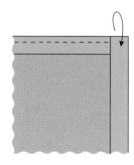

9. Repeat in the same manner at all corners. Stop sewing several inches from where you started stitching the binding to the quilt.

10. Join the ends of the binding by folding the ending binding tail back on itself where it meets the beginning of the binding. From the fold, measure and mark the cut width (2⅛") of your binding strip. Cut the ending binding tail to this measurement.

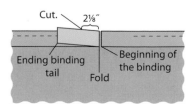

Cut. 2⅛"

Ending binding tail

Fold

Beginning of the binding

11. Open both tails. Place one tail on top of the other at a right angle, right sides together. Mark a diagonal line, and stitch on the line. Trim the seam allowance to ¼". Press the seam open. Refold the binding strip, and finish stitching it to the quilt.

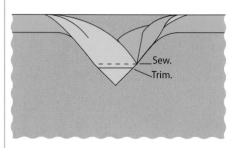

Sew.
Trim.

12. Turn the folded edge of the binding over the raw edge of the quilt, and slip-stitch the binding to the backing. Form miters at the corners.

quilt label

I always encourage quiltmakers to label their quilts. The information you include on the label will be treasured for generations to come. Use a permanent fabric pen on the back (or even on the front) of the quilt, or design a beautiful patch specifically for the quilt with embroidery or colorful fabric pens. Before sewing the label to the quilt, consider also writing directly on the quilt (where the label will cover) to ensure that the information will not be lost if the label is removed.

Resources

Bernina (of America)
(630) 978-2500
www.bernina.com

Superior Threads
Libby Lehman's The Bottom Line and
Alex Anderson's MasterPiece fine cotton thread
(800) 499-1777
www.superiorthreads.com

Roxanne International
Roxanne's Glue Baste-It
(800) 993-4445
www.thatperfectstitch.com

The Warm Company
Steam-A-Seam 2
(425) 248-2424
www.warmcompany.com

Prym Consumer USA
Fray Check
www.dritz.com

Hobbico
Hobbico Craft Iron
www.hobbico.com

Alex Anderson's 4-in-1 Essential Sewing Tool (C&T)

Quilter's Freezer Paper (C&T)

Quilter's Vinyl (C&T)

About *the* Author

Alex Anderson's love affair with quiltmaking began in 1978, when she completed her *Grandmother's Flower Garden* quilt as part of her work toward a degree in art at San Francisco State University. Over the years, her focus has rested on understanding fabric relationships and on an intense appreciation for traditional quilting surface design and star quilts.

Alex's mission is to educate, inspire, entertain, and grow today's quilting community. With this mission in mind, she has had the privilege and pleasure of ushering tens of thousands of new people into the world of quilting. For eleven years, she hosted television's premier quilt show, *Simply Quilts*, and she is currently the co-host and an executive producer of *The Quilt Show* with Ricky Tims (www.thequiltshow.com), an interactive website that features full production videos and is connecting quilters worldwide.

When Alex is not traveling, she resides in Northern California with her husband and a new kitty and faces daily the challenges of feeding various forms of wildlife in her backyard. Visit her website at www.alexandersonquilts.com.

OTHER BOOKS BY ALEX ANDERSON

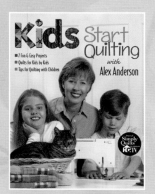
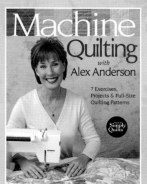

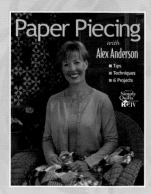

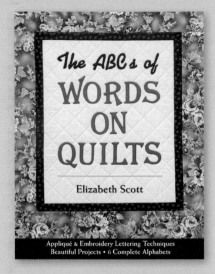

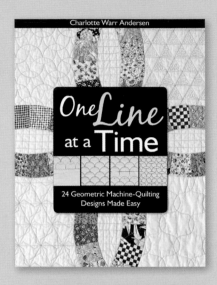